PROUD TO SAY THAT NAME
The Marble Hall of Fame

AMY LAWRENCE

MAINSTREAM PUBLISHING

EDINBURGH AND LONDON

FOOTBALL

First published in 1997 by
MAINSTREAM PUBLISHING COMPANY
(EDINBURGH) LTD
7 Albany Street
Edinburgh EH1 3UG

ISBN 1 85158 898 1

A catalogue record for this book is available from the
British Library

Typeset in Adobe Garamond and Gill Sans
Printed and bound in Great Britain by Butler & Tanner Ltd

Contents

To Richard, for the Littlewoods Cup Final ticket in 1987
Matty, for covering for me on 26 May 1989
Eugene and Mark, for knowing what it means

Acknowledgements

Heartfelt thanks to George Graham, George Armstrong, Frank McLintock, Charlie George, Pat Rice, Liam Brady, Kenny Sansom, David Rocastle, Ian Wright, Tony Adams, David Seaman and Dennis Bergkamp for their time, their thoughts, their inspiration and all the joy they have given us over the years. I am also indebted to Don Howe, Bob Wilson and Alan Smith for their willing memories and enthusiasm, and to David Dein and Ken Friar for their help and encouragement. I owe hefty favours to Iain Cook for answering every anorak poser I could dream up and to Clare Tomlinson and Amanda Docherty for coping with my phone pest persona. I'm eternally grateful to Arsenal sages Tom Watt and Eugene Harper for such fantastic support and advice; to Tony Madden and Dave Bissmire for the reference material; to Andy Heap for helping me find a way forward when I was stuck in reverse.

Thanks, too, to Michael Marks for taking me to my first game; Rosemary Roots for teaching me to write and having patience when I was a wayward horror; Patrick Barclay for being a guru; Olivia Blair, my soul sister in every which way but one; and Grandma for learning to love football.

Much gratitude to Bill Campbell, Peter Mackenzie, Judy Diamond and all at Mainstream for letting me loose on a subject so dear to my heart, and the *Observer* sportsdesk for under-standing my distraction.

And cheers to everyone in the Arsenal family.

For permission to reproduce photographs, thanks to Allsport, Press Association, Mirror Syndication International, Bill Smith and Doug Poole.

Amy Lawrence
London N5
August 1997

Introduction

On 26 May 1989 I kissed more men in one night than I have in 26 years of life. Most of them smelt of beer and sweaty polyester. Many had clearly not been blessed in the beauty department. And yet I kissed them all, with unreasonably deep emotion. The visitors' terrace at Anfield hosted the kind of uninhibited, free love not seen since Woodstock in 1969. Or maybe Anderlecht in 1970.

It's about belonging to the Arsenal family. It's about looking into a stranger's face and seeing an expression that mirrors your own feelings. It's about empathy, and knowing the rest of the universe is willing you to get stuffed at every available opportunity. It's about sharing the moment. Four thousand of us in Liverpool swam in an ocean of joy, carried through the ebb and flow of the crowd as we floated round embracing as many people as we could get our hands on. Male and female, black and white, kids and pensioners, affluent and skint, all part of the Highbury tribe.

Certain faces remain imprinted on my memory. A 15-stone skinhead who was blubbing like a baby, and a stubbly Irishman whose eyes glazed over as if he was in Never-Never-Land, whispering, 'It's my birthday,' over and over again. Other than a fondness for Arsenal, I knew nothing whatsoever about either of them.

Not even a name. And we all hugged with the ardour of long-lost siblings. That instant bond and unconditional belonging is one of the reasons football intoxicates. From my first game at the age of six I was wowed by this gathering of a multitude of strangers who, somehow, were all mates.

I remember trying to explain this phenomenon to people who had no interest in the game. At school on Monday mornings, I regaled the girls with tales of my weekend exploits and new pals. They walked away yawning and sneering, finding the whole concept both unfathomable and unappealing. Which was precisely my reaction to Saturday-afternoon mooching round shops pondering over some new shade of lip gloss. Yeah, life-altering experience. Most of them had never been as far as Watford. Let alone a trip to Nirvana via Liverpool. Or an adventure in Coventry's urban jungle, avoiding ambush on the perilous route from Highfield Road back to the station. I could feel my heart drumming in between my ears – you don't get that at Miss Selfridge. Nor do you want to leap into the arms of the nearest person in recognition of a shared passion for Calvin Klein.

The game can elicit irrational emotions not only towards your fellow fans and worshipped players, but to anyone who aids the cause. Take that night at Anfield for instance. Alan Smith heads the ball past Bruce Grobbelaar and Liverpool hound the referee, urging him to disallow the strike. He goes to speak to his linesman . . . I have a fixation with that linesman. It strikes me as shameful bordering on tragic that I should be fixated by a middle-aged man with a big nose and a wispy moustache and a yellow flag (I have no further details) yet every time I watch the video and lipread those words he says to the ref – *It was a goal* – I come over all goosepimply and want to throw my arms around him and give him a box of Roses. It's inexplicable, and slightly worrying, but there you have it. That's what football, and Arsenal in particular, did to me. From time to time I have spouted thoughts I ought not, uttered words better left unsaid, and acted abominably. And it's all been okay because I'm amongst my own.

★

While I was writing this book, flicking through match pro-
grammes from 1971, I stumbled upon a eulogy to the club
penned by erstwhile editor Harry Homer. It encapsulates
everything about the Highbury kinship: 'Together we form a
great family and Arsenal is our tie. We are Denis Hill-Wood our
chairman, and his son Peter, and his grandfather the late Sir
Samuel, who was called with affection "Sir Sam" in the dressing-
room during the '30s. We are the Man on the Spot who always
stood on the same position behind the Laundry goal and wrote
me encouraging letters when things were going badly. We are
Tom Parker, Charlie Buchan, Eddie Hapgood and Joe Mercer –
Arsenal captains who have been my friends . . . We are a Spanish
friend who has ended every letter for more than 20 years with a
cheer for Bilbao's Athletic and one for London's Arsenal. We are
directors, the doctor, stewards and staff; gate men, St John's men,
commissionaires and police; trainers, the scouts, and the players
– these last our family's pride.'

Twenty-six years later: new names, same spirit. We are David
Dein and Ken Friar, head honchos guiding the club into the 21st
century. We are Bondholders who forked out £1,500 to stay on
the North Bank and Junior Gunners who are enrolled by their
parents 20 minutes after their birth. We are Frank McLintock and
Tony Adams, skippers whose leadership qualities would win the
respect of the captains of yesteryear. We are Pat Rice, George
Armstrong, Liam Brady, Don Howe, David Court and Paul
Davis, former players who still work at Highbury. We are George
Graham and David Rocastle, Arsenal men wherever they may
roam. We are physios, masseurs and dieticians; the bloke who
used to weave through the terraces hawking peanuts; the fans who
queue up for bagels at half-time. We are executive-box holders
and regulars in the disabled section. We are Gary, Markus and
Matthew phoning from Holland, Sweden and New York for the
latest on the Arsenal's fortunes. We are Cliff Bastin and Ian
Wright; Herbert Chapman and Arsène Wenger. Times change but
the family lives on.

In compiling a fantasy XI for this book one of my criteria was
that they are Arsenal men. Players who represent more than their
own talent and effort, they also convey the soul of the club. They

are, as the song goes, proud to say that name. Not that this measure made the task of picking a team of heroes a great deal easier. In fact I spent months in a state of flummoxed confusion, dropping and reinstating players like a chronically unco-ordinated juggler.

A few years ago there was an outlandish television series called *The Manageress*, about football's first woman boss, and I remember tutting at her crass notions and claiming I could do a better job. I now realise I could never be a manageress, considering my club would be halfway through the season by the time I had selected the team. And if indecision isn't a serious enough managerial flaw, an excess of female sympathy makes me entirely unsuitable for the vocation. Oh, the guilt trip I put myself through over leaving out David O'Leary, Peter Storey and Alan Smith. Utter mental torment. I elected to entrust the business of being ruthless to the men who know best. Therefore George Graham was my obvious choice to manage the players.

Now to construct a team for him. Since this book is about reliving Arsenal highlights through the men who made them, I plumped for the 1970 Fairs Cup as the natural starting point. I thought it unfair to go back any further in time, out of respect for players who are no longer with us and could only be contacted via a medium, which is a tad too impractical. It was also necessary to manipulate the team in order to find a balance of players from each successful era, hence a number of Arsenal greats are undeservedly confined to the reserves. An alternative team sheet might read Wilson, Dixon, McNab, O'Leary, Simpson, Rix, Storey, Davis, Merson, Radford, Smith. Which still leaves Jennings, Bould, Thomas, Limpar and Macdonald on the bench . . . True to the spirit of the Arsenal family, and saluting everyone who has played his part, each chapter leads off with full line-ups from the club's memorable triumphs.

Eventually I whittled it down to an XI which embodies all of Arsenal's traditions at their finest: an exceptional defence consisting of a masterful keeper and four captains who take each goal conceded as the ultimate insult; a midfield boasting brain, brawn and brio who appreciate the balance between entertaining and winning; and a spellbinding front two who strike the fear of God into any opposition. Importantly, it's a team who will work for each other as well as themselves. A group capable of generating a togetherness which means the whole outweighs the sum of its parts. No doubt they won't get the credit they deserve outside Highbury and they will be called boring and lucky when they have an off day, but I fancy this lot could perform a few miracles, fashion a few last-minute winners, and keep the door of the trophy cabinet ajar.

I make no excuses if I occasionally slip into hagiography, and offer no pretence that this is a thoughtfully argued, well-balanced appraisal of three decades of Arsenal Football Club. The aim is to celebrate the good times. Thanks to the men who tell the stories in this tome, there have been plenty. Let them roll.

I'm Having That

GEORGE GRAHAM

Liverpool 0 Arsenal 2
26 May 1989

Lukic, Dixon, Winterburn, Thomas, O'Leary, Adams, Rocastle, Richardson, Smith, Bould (Groves), Merson (Hayes)

Standing in his study, his face a mere inch from a framed print of the 1990–91 league table, George Graham stares and stares at the statistics. Played 38, won 24, drew 13, lost 1. There it is in history for ever: lost one. You can almost see the brainstorming session going on inside his head . . . *Only one defeat, incredible . . . Two points deducted as well . . . And Tony Adams's time away . . . Still managed 24 clean sheets . . . Anders Limpar, och Anders Limpar . . .* George eases into a smug smile. He had glided over every hurdle and finished in record-breaking style. His icon, Herbert Chapman, whom he would occasionally wink at while swanning through the Marble Halls, would have been mighty impressed with that one. The evening the Championship was won, a banner was hung from the East Stand, simply stating 'George knows', which summed up the way the Highbury hordes felt about their modern-day overlord. Just as the word of Chapman had been creed, the word of George was gospel. Arsenal had absolute faith in his judgement.

For a while, nobody dreamed of questioning his moves, even if some of them looked mysterious. Two years on, Anders Limpar was doing a passable impression of the invisible man. Pal Lydersen was getting games. So was Jimmy Carter. And Arsenal finished a disagreeable tenth in the league, having scored a feeble 40 goals as they slogged along.

Selective memory is a curious thing. Highbury's resident pessimists began to grumble and groan and gripe. Optimists thought they had to be insane. Yes, an indistinguishable mass of 0–0 draws and 0–1 defeats popped rather too many braincells, but surely two sparky Cup runs more than compensated. George still knew. After all, here were Arsenal aiming for the first ever domestic Cup Double. Another slice of history, eh, Herbert?

At Wembley the non-believers were left wondering how they could ever have doubted their leader, forgetting their moans to hum along with the celebratory chant: 'Oh, Georgie Graham's magic, he wears a magic hat, and when he saw the FA Cup he said, *I'm having that.*' During the Graham era, the song was a hit in various forms, the line about the FA Cup replaced by the Championship or the Cup-Winners' Cup, but the theme remained the same: Georgie Graham's magic hat made everything he touched turn to silver. He could, it appeared, have whatever he wanted. And he wanted every trophy going. Here was a man who had an insatiable appetite, and to Arsenal's astonishment he found a way to satisfy it year after year. No sooner had he drank a cup of joy than he was craving the next gulp. His thirst seemed all the more amazing set against the seven-year drought which the club had endured. Prior to George's arrival, the closest thing resembling an Arsenal success was Charlie Nicholas's reputation with the ladies.

In the close-season of 1986, the Bonnie Prince witnessed the entrance of a Scot who was also once a renowned Highbury hedonist, but if Champagne Charlie thought his new manager would clink glasses with him and smile with nostalgic empathy at his Stringfellows lifestyle, he was wrong.

'For Christ's sake, put the ball away and give us a vodka and coke.' These were the words of the Stroller, the suavest of swingers whose mind switched off football as soon as he left the pitch. George would scoff as his 1971 team-mates tore into a heated critique of some match or other; the only strikers he cared to discuss had catwalk legs, billowing hair and could melt the hearts of Norman Hunter, Ron Harris and Nobby Stiles put together. No, not Charlie George.

The George Graham who swept back into Arsenal was no longer a playboy; he was a workaholic, and he meant business. He was so absorbed by football, so obsessed by winning, that he spoke and thought of little else. All outside concerns, including his marriage, fought a losing battle for his attention. George is consumed by one aim: to win the trophies which would rank him next to Arsenal's greatest manager, Herbert Chapman. Stroller now seems to be a misnomer; instead, words like 'stern' and 'steely' and 'strict' shadow his every step. He had become a man with different priorities. For Christ's sake, put the vodka and coke away and give us a magnum of champagne.

In his quest to taste glory, George was a stickler for detail, and he demanded total dedication and discipline from his new squad. During his first pep talk at the training ground at London Colney, George wasted no time showing his intentions. Noticing that Nicholas and Graham Rix had pierced ears underneath their bouffant footballer haircuts, he quipped, 'If you want to wear an earring it's compulsory to wear a dress. Wear it socially, no problem, but don't come to work in an earring.' It was typical George, authoritative yet audacious. A flash of quick wit to make his point with a bit of punch. He wasn't going to lay down the rules like an old fuddy-duddy, but he made it clear there was to be *no messing*.

George introduced a code of conduct: the Arsenal blazer and tie and grey flannel trousers would be worn on all official duties. Behaviour was to be equally smart – no more front-page incidents now, boys (well, that was the idea). As for behaviour on the pitch, everyone in the squad was on trial. Over the next six weeks he would make decisions about who would stay and who would go. 'I'm going to do things my way,' he emphasised. 'It may not be everyone else's way, but it's my way.'

The players, as groups of players do, sat on the grass and said nothing. 'I think they thought: "We've heard it all before, we'll see how good you are." I knew from then on they would be judging me every single time I was with them,' George recalls. 'Footballers may not be the brightest academically, but streetwise they're red hot.' The task of winning their respect hardly over-awed the new boss. After all, he was a man who had called in the army to clear the stadium of rampaging fans when he was manager of Millwall. No problem would have George running scared.

The army incident, just another solution he found to what was a maze of conundrums at the Den, had been clocked by one or two wise heads at Arsenal. Without deliberately keeping track of a prodigal Highbury son, George's progress impressed the directors. With the hot seat vacant, he was invited to Peter Hill-Wood's apartment for an interview with the chairman, vice-chairman David Dein and managing director Ken Friar. They had a shortlist of four but it was decided to approach Graham first. 'The fact there was an Arsenal connection carried a lot of weight,' explains Dein. 'He had Arsenal in his heart and we thought that meant something.' George's charm and ambition impressed so much the other three candidates were never approached.

Buoyed by the feeling he had crammed ten years of mana-gerial experience into three and a half seasons at Millwall, George oozed confidence. He couldn't guarantee he would shake Arsenal out of their apathy, but he could assure the directors he would dive headlong, without a second's hesitation, into the challenge. 'I was very excited. I think anything in life that's important to you should get the adrenaline pumping, and mine sure was. I do promise *commitment, desire, passion*,' he spits the words out. 'I don't overestimate my abilities. I got into football management knowing full well you have to be successful and that if you're not you're going to get the sack. Nobody gets the sack if they finish in the top three or qualify for Europe . . . except Bruce Rioch.' George giggles mischievously.

In his first season, George's Arsenal finished outside the top three and didn't qualify for Europe. Okay, that's a cheap shot. It was in fact a season of remarkable highs, enough to make every-one giddy with elation and expectation they had clean forgotten how to feel. The Gunners took pole position in the league from November to February, won the Littlewoods Cup, and registered three, yes three, victories at White Hart Lane. Joy unbridled.

When David Rocastle swung a left foot in the 300th minute of a momentous semi-final to complete a colossal comeback against the team from the wrong end of Seven Sisters Road, taking Arsenal to Wembley into the bargain, the basis for what made the Graham era so successful was crystallised: never-say-die spirit, a collective belief which could overwhelm technically superior opponents, the ability to steal the jewels from someone else's home, and a knack for those devastating last-minute goals. The sight of George's boys jigging and hugging and kissing each other while Tottenham fans tore up their Cup Final coupons spoke volumes. At that precise moment it was clear the 11 individuals who had been trotting out in red and white before George had become a team.

'When I arrived I looked at the staff and sadly there were three groups: the recognised stars, and of the young diamonds there was a split between the black boys and the white boys. I knew from my playing career at Arsenal that they've all got to have one target, one aim,' George declares. If he was going to be a winner, the players had to be winners. He drummed into them what could be achieved and, as shared ambition grew, so the factions evaporated.

Perspiration on the training field was the key to Graham's winning formula. 'I absolutely love training,' he says. And didn't the players know it. From day one, his priority was to organise the defence. The monotony of repeating the same routines *ad nauseam* might have bored the pants off David O'Leary, Tony Adams, Kenny Sansom and Viv Anderson, but for George it was a daily fix. He practised with his back four until they clicked like a metronome, a sight he found hypnotic. 'I love the challenge, planning something and getting it organised. Even the bulbs in my garden are in formation.'

Just as, 17 years before, his own manager Bertie Mee had sparked an Arsenal revival by blending the older pros with the willingness and fearlessness of youth, so did George. He inherited from Don Howe half a team's worth of teenage dreams – Tony Adams, David Rocastle, Mickey Thomas, Paul Merson, Niall Quinn, Martin Hayes and, er, Gus Caesar – and there was no gentle cosseting, no wimpy rests. If they were good enough, they were old enough, and they were playing.

'We topped the table for *12 weeks!*' gasps George, as if he still can't believe it ten years later, 'and that was with people like Quinny, Hayesy, Grovesy and Charlie in attack. I was working them hard in training, not physically but tactically. I kept saying we had no chance of winning the league. The press were getting fed up with me – they thought it was a gimmick. It was, to take the pressure off the young players. There was experience at the back and in midfield but I always thought we weren't strong enough up front.' George got the best out of Niall Quinn, the Irish behemoth, and Martin Hayes, the sprightly tryer with an eye for goal (well, for one season anyway), but he wanted better. He had his eye on another big man–small man partnership, Alan Smith and Paul Merson. 'Those 12 weeks were fantastic and the Cup was the icing on the cake. I thought, *Hmm, a few more players and this could be good.'*

The first act of Graham's tenure had exceeded the hopes of a super-optimist, and now he chased even loftier dreams. Few anticipated such a brave new world would evolve when he made his first signing for the club, Perry Groves, a £75,000 winger from Colchester. Few realised how that symbolised George's transfer style, a method which would serve him so well for seasons to come. He bought cheaply from smaller clubs, players who fought for the right to perform on one of the great stages in English football, players who had something to prove, players whose egos were not monsters which couldn't be moulded by Graham: Alan Smith, Nigel Winterburn, Lee Dixon, Steve Bould, Brian Marwood – all would become champions quicker than you could say, *We won the league on Merseyside.*

14 January 1989. Everton away. As the two teams leave the field, 30,000 blue fans at Goodison Park are on their feet applauding what they have just witnessed. Only the cheers are not directed towards the Toffeemen but at the rampant visitors who had given them a good hiding. It's a goosepimply moment for Arsenal, who have grown to expect insults on their travels, not standing ovations. The fact that Everton supporters had watched a team which looked set to take the title from their rivals Liverpool may have had something to do with their sporting generosity but, nevertheless, they had seen their team win the league twice in the previous four years and knew all about champion credentials. They recognised all the hallmarks in Arsenal. Leading the First Division, and peering confidently over their shoulders at an imposing gap they had worked so hard to create, the team which George built looked unstoppable. John Lukic kept flapping to a minimum to have his most consistent season in an Arsenal jersey; Dixon and Winterburn slotted into the back four, invigorating replacements for Anderson and Sansom; Marwood and Rocastle tore up and down the country's wings, cajoling and crossing with pace and precision; and the Smith–Merson double act, with its combination of experience and impudence, yielded goals aplenty.

Away from home in particular, George's revolution turned Arsenal into a revelation. In fact their record away from Highbury was superior to form on home soil. As well as the Everton show, Wimbledon succumbed 5–1 at Plough Lane, and at the City Ground, Nottingham Forest's classic counter-attackers were beaten 4–1 at their own game. By April, though, having jittered and frittered away what had seemed like an unassailable advantage over their challengers, Arsenal faced two trips which were crucial to shaping the season's destiny, to the two most notoriously daunting grounds: Old Trafford and Anfield.

2 April. Manchester United away. These are the facts. One – Arsenal adopted the sweeper system. Two – in the driving rain, Tony Adams flung his head amongst the flailing boots to give Arsenal the lead on 78 minutes. Three – Tony Adams flung his leg at a United cross to slice the ball past Lukic on 85 minutes. This is the fiction: One – 'Arsenal seemed to have reverted to their old boring, boring image at Old Trafford where George Graham fielded three centre-backs' (*The Independent*). Two – 'EE AW!' (*The Mirror*). Three – Donkey's ears thoughtfully superimposed over a picture of our Tone. (*The Mirror*).

This is George's view of events: 'We deserved to win that night. The press gave me a right hard time at Old Trafford. I was hammered the next day, "Graham's bottle's gone" and "Graham's gone defensive". They all said I went there with five at the back but it was 3-5-2 and I played it for a reason. The purpose, albeit I didn't know it was going to be the last game of the season, was to beat *Liverpool.* They were the cream then. They had Barnes on one flank, Houghton on the other, Rushie up front. I thought, if I let them get the ball and run at us they'll destroy us. So I made it competitive: I put Lee Dixon right on top of Barnes, pushed Nigel Winterburn right on top of Houghton, had Tony and Bouldy marking and David O'Leary sweeping up. He was perfect for the role and he should be thankful for it – it was only because of that system that he got more medals in the last couple of years of his career than he'd ever had in his life!

'I remember a couple of weeks before Old Trafford saying to the lads, "I'm going to change the system from 4-4-2 to 3-5-2." They all looked at me. We're top of the league and they're saying, "Why are we changing?" That was a difficult one. I thought, I hope they don't lose confidence in me. We worked on it in training, playing that system against the youth team, all specially designed to take on Liverpool. All that media now, going on about the new three-at-the-back system which half the teams in the Premier Division are now playing; I played it in 1989 and was crucified for it.'

23 April. Liverpool away. Cancelled. It was a sunny afternoon on Merseyside, thousands of fans were gathered, queuing to get into Anfield. Only they weren't there to watch a match, they were there to pay their respects to their fallen, fellow football lovers, to see the Kop covered in scarves and flowers. Eight days before, 96 Liverpool fans were killed in a crush on the Leppings Lane terrace at Hillsborough. They had gone to Sheffield to watch their team play an FA Cup semi-final against Nottingham Forest and never returned. May they rest in peace.

Merseyside mourned, and a part of every fan in the country grieved with them. The business of getting back to football was difficult to fathom. Nobody wanted to address the question of whether the 1989 FA Cup and Championship should be aborted. Nobody could work out whether the game meant anything any more. It was a particularly complex issue for Forest, Liverpool's Cup opponents, and Arsenal, Liverpool's rivals for the title. The Reds decided to continue.

'Hillsborough had a big impact on me,' George reflects. 'Finally, Bill Shankly's saying was laid to rest. Football is not more important than life and death. *It is not.* For the passionate people of Merseyside, all of football felt for them. It's impossible to know how they really feel. You'll never know their pain, suffering, sorrow. You're sympathetic but you don't know how the families really feel.' In terms of returning to football, Arsenal took their lead from Liverpool; only when they were ready to pick up the tempo would everyone else follow suit. 'Kenny Dalglish and the players handled it superbly. They got it out their system. One of the ways of getting through traumas is to keep yourself busy, with no time to think. They just took off and went on a great run.'

To Liverpool's credit, they continued where they had left off, in seemingly invincible form, which culminated in a 24-match unbeaten run to take them into the last match of the season, that rescheduled match against Arsenal. Had George's boys not stumbled at the penultimate hurdle, the game would have been meaningless, just a case of completing the season's fixtures. But Derby County and Wimbledon came to Highbury and did the unthinkable: they had the sheer cheek to take five points from the champions elect. 'Highburied!' cried *The People.* 'Blown it!' screamed *The Mirror.* Gimme a quadruple vodka, blubbed the Arsenal faithful. At the end of the final home match of the season, the players trooped round on a lap of honour, symbolically suggesting the game was up.

'I thought maybe it just wasn't meant to be,' George recalls. 'But one of my philosophies is that if you're going down [he pauses, his voice drops dramatically] go down *fighting, scratching, biting, kicking.* I love people having a go even if they're getting beaten. Have a go! Don't give in too easily, fight it all the way.'

That fight, according to everyone without red and white cannons rolling through their veins, would be heavyweights against featherweights. Arsenal should have known better than to expect any kind of favour from West Ham, Liverpool's weedy opponents three days before the grandest of finales. 5–1, five bloody one, and the scene was set. The pessimists sank into dark gloom; the optimists sounded like modern-day members of the

Light Brigade; the mathematicians concluded George's boys had to win by two clear goals to claim the Championship. That way they would be level on points, level on goal difference, and ahead by the most minute of margins (ironically enough for boring, boring Arsenal): goals scored. 'You don't have a prayer, Arsenal,' mocked our friends at *The Mirror*.

It was just the goading to get George's goat. 'I don't know what it is – maybe it's part of my make up. I said, "Look lads, we know what we've got to do. Let's get up there and do it, as simple as that. The lovely thing is, nobody expects us to do it. Nobody. Only within Highbury. What have we got to lose? Nothing. There's no pressure on us at all." I really believed that.' To suggest nobody expected Arsenal to do it is akin to reminding the citizens of Rome of the Pope's religion.

The week before the game was so relaxed it was a surprise George didn't replace training with yoga sessions. He knew the tension would mount as soon as the team arrived at Fortress Anfield, but it would be jokes all the way there to keep confidence bubbling. He was following primal instincts, lessons learned from a book he much admires, *The Naked Ape* by Desmond Morris.

'It's the story about the ape and its similarities with the human race,' explains George. 'The apes fight when you go into their territory. I always used to relate it to football. When you go to somewhere like Liverpool, a hostile environment, their attitude is: "What are you doing up here? You're wasting your time. Why don't you get away back home again? You are going to get murdered tomorrow." In a team you're going to get some weak and some strong characters. The strong ones are fine. *Yeah, come on! We'll take you on.* Some are not as strong mentally, and the longer you are in that environment, the lower the weaker ones sink. I'm a great believer that when you're going into enemy territory, get in there like a raid. Do the damage and get back out again.'

Arsenal duly travelled to Merseyside on the day of the game – no point spending any longer than necessary in alien surroundings. The squad paused for a meal and a stretch and a team-talk in a local hotel to prepare, mentally and physically, for the charge. As Tony Adams recalls, George put the football away, brought out the crystal ball, and came into his own. 'The belief he had was just amazing. He read the script before the game! He told us the result, how we were going to score and everything. Bloody amazing. Possessed.' Keep it tight at the back, he said (would you believe). Don't go rampaging forward recklessly, he warned. Nil-nil at half-time will be fine, then we'll score early in the second half and nick one at the death, he concluded. Uncanny. We realise 'George knows' but that is ridiculous.

Did you honestly say that, George? 'Yes, that's the truth. I convinced the boys, it was superb. I'll always remember sitting in that hotel thinking, I wonder if they believe me? I wonder if I've bullshitted enough here?' He slaps his thigh and booms with laughter.

By the looks on their faces did you really think you'd convinced them, George? 'No, they thought, "He must be mad."' His eyes widen and glow.

Did you truly believe it would happen, George? 'Actually,' he confesses, 'I did predict 3–0. I thought we'd get the second one a little earlier and then we'd nick another one.' He looks deadly serious, believe me.

The team's response symbolised the carefree mood, as David Rocastle remembers. 'The boys were thinking, Yeah, all right, George, just take that bottle of brandy out your pocket, will yer?'

Inside the stadium, the FA Cup, secured six days before, is ready and ribboned, close at hand so Anfield could salute the Double at the final whistle. Everybody connected with Liverpool Football Club thinks there is more chance of the Mersey drying out than the Championship trophy leaving town. Old boy Graeme Souness had written a considered article in *The Sun*, headlined 'Men Against Boys', running though the individual battles and explaining why Liverpool would win each and every one. George pins it up on the noticeboard in the dressing-room. 'It was good, it helped me motivate the lads. I should have sent Graeme a bottle of champagne,' he chuckles.

Never before had English football witnessed a climax like this – it was like the FA Cup Final and league rolled into one. The 90 other teams had completed their fixtures and, like fascinated voyeurs, watch the only outstanding 90 minutes of the season unfold. Both teams have one hand on the trophy (even if Liverpool's is vice-like and Arsenal's slippery). 'A night of chilling simplicity,' intones Brian Moore. Waves of emotion still rolling after Hillsborough create a unique atmosphere – the result simultaneously means everything and nothing – and as a gesture to the memory of those who weren't there, the visitors take to the field bearing bouquets of flowers to give to the Liverpool supporters who were.

At half-time, just as George had foreseen, it's 0–0 and phase one of the masterplan is completed. Arsenal are inadvertently aided by Kenny Dalglish's tactics: knowing a draw or even a 1–0 defeat would suffice, the Reds play it cool, protecting the advantage they had going into the game. 'They didn't attack us as much as they should have done. They weren't in a rush to score but if they *had* scored, I don't think we would have won it,' George reveals. Seven minutes into the second half, time for phase two of the plan. Play Brian Moore: 'Arsenal's free-kick, Winterburn and Richardson behind it. Adams has made a darting little run in there . . . AND SMITH! AND ARSENAL HAVE SCORED!'

The instant the ball is delicately glanced past Grobbelaar, a gang of Liverpool players home in on the referee David Hutchinson like children in a collective tantrum. He consults his linesman. 'I was very disappointed both in the officials and in Liverpool because it was a good goal,' reflects George. 'Liverpool hesitated: *They've not scored have they?* The first thing they thought was *He must have been offside, let's run to the linesman.* I thought the pressure might have got to the referee and he may have switched his decision. It's modern football – everybody appeals. It was just the way they appealed *en masse*, surrounding the referee. I think it was a token gesture.'

Liverpool, it later transpires, claimed Smith didn't get a touch on what was an indirect free-kick, although television replays, along with the mud mark which the ball painted on Smudger's face, prove conclusive. 'I couldn't work out why they were appealing and when the ref pointed to the centre spot I thought, "Well done, you've been strong there,"' says Smith. 'I was on a high to have scored in such a massive game, but it was still a mountain to climb to get the second.'

Then, the moment the Gunners had been dreaming about for 18 years. Chances had been as rare as Arsenal triumphs at Liverpool and there is Mickey Thomas face to face with Bruce Grobbelaar, the destiny of the Championship in his right boot. He toe-pokes it straight at the Liverpool keeper. Phase three foiled.

George sees his prediction crumbling before his very eyes. 'I says, "Oh no, we're not going to score three now." Honestly, I thought we'd given it a good go even if we won 1–0. We were magnificent. I was proud of the players.' While Arsenal are beating Liverpool, time, it seems, is beating the Gunners. Analyst David Pleat witters on about poetic justice, as if the brave challengers deserve to come within one frigging goal of the title. One goal! Be still my beating blood pressure. The 12 million TV audience watch the seconds tick by on a yellow clock in the corner of the screen.

Caught up in the mesmeric mood inside Anfield, time beats to an illusory rhythm. When Kevin Richardson lies on the turf with acute cramp, felled by his own efforts, David Rocastle thinks there's 20 minutes to go. That's 19 more than Steve McMahon's calculations then. 'Champions,' sing the Kop, and to be fair to them, at that moment they still are. George isn't aware of the time, except for a feeling that it is fading away. In the corner of his eye he sees Dalglish shouting, 'Barnesey, run it towards the corner flag,' the age-old symbol of timewasting, just keeping possession until the final whistle. Except Barnsey doesn't run it towards the corner flag, he meanders into the area and gets dispossessed by Richardson, who passes the ball straight into the arms of John Lukic: 91 minutes on the clock.

A poser for you. You are the goalkeeper, it's injury-time and the crowd is whistling, coaxing the referee to join their tune, but your team needs one more goal. Do you (a) hoof the ball as far up the field as you can to launch an attack, or (b) calmly throw it to your full-back? Play Brian Moore: 'And Arsenal come streaming forward now in surely what will be their last attack. A good ball by Dixon, finding Smith, to Thomas, charging through the midfield. THOMAS. IT'S UP FOR GRABS NOOWWW! THOMAS!!'

Ecstasy. A dozen tabs of pure MDMA could never do for anyone what that moment does for every Arsenal man, woman and child. Briefly, we are all transported to Eden. 'It was just like a dream,' whispers George. 'In fact, I was in so much of a dreamlike state I never even jumped up. I just sat there, with everyone leaping around me. It was incredible. There's a saying that you have three moments in your life which are magical, mystical, can never be repeated. Anfield is one of mine, without question.' Bloody hell, George, your other two must have been good.

'There was only one man to take that shot,' believes David Rocastle, best friend of the coolest man in the stadium. But Rocky, remember, is somewhere between paradise and panic as there are 19 minutes to go in his head. 'The boys were all doing their somersaults and I thought, I'm not getting involved in this, I'm saving my energy because Liverpool are going to *attack, attack, attack*. So when Mickey came back to the halfway line I just winked at him. I asked the ref how long and he said, "That's about it, 25 seconds." I didn't believe him – I'm surprised he didn't book me for my reaction. Then I started shaking, Jesus, we're 25 seconds away from winning the Championship, I had to pull myself together.' No one is more together than Mickey, who has the composure to pop up in defence to serenely caress the ball back to Lukic in those final seconds. You could smoke all the grass in the world and you wouldn't be that chilled.

The Mirror, having damned Arsenal so often during the season, headlined with 'The Greatest Story Ever Told'. The captain, whom they had portrayed as a donkey, was a champion. 'As soon as that final whistle went, I fell to my knees,' says Adams. 'The emotion was frightening, it just knocked my feet away from me. I was immobilised by it. It was one of those beautiful, beautiful moments that will be with me for the rest of my life.'

And all along, George knew. He knew it was going to happen that sublime way. All his managerial strategies and idiosyncrasies came together on 26 May 1989. The man who wanted to rule the world of Arsenal earned a new name. The tabloids christened him 'King George'. The fans went for something more spiritual than regal, 'The Messiah'.

Back in his study, he gets the shivers when he looks at one particular photograph of himself gripping the trophy that night. It captures more than a moment. He is dressed in the Arsenal blazer and tie and grey flannel trousers (and none of his players wore earrings or a dress); he is on the move, walking past the infamous 'This is Anfield' sign (the naked ape sneaking successfully out of his enemy's territory) and his eyes, eyes which saw the plot he wrote enacted for real, are on stalks.

It could have been so very different. Lukic might not have thrown that ball out to Dixon, Thomas might not have even played if Paul Davis hadn't missed a large chunk of the season after flattening Southampton's Glen Cockerill, and Anfield might not have mattered if Arsenal hadn't self-destructed in the penultimate week of the season. 'If we had beaten Derby and Wimbledon we could have won it without Anfield,' smiles George, 'but that chase was the script – it wasn't the script I wrote, it was probably the work of the Roy of the Rovers creator.' Would he have preferred it any other way? George thinks that is the most ridiculous question he has ever heard. 'I'd have rather already won it and enjoyed the last one at Anfield, are you kidding? Let's enjoy life!'

Planned or predestined? 'I honestly believe it was meant to be. I believe in fate as long as you give it your best shot. I don't think you can sit back, not work and say, "It's meant to be." That's nonsense. You've got to give it everything you've got and the players did that all through the season. I drove them hard. I'm a very demanding person, I set high standards. You're not appreciated as much at the time as you are a few years later, when the players realise what they really achieved and how much they responded, how much work they put in, how much I pushed them. I was not easy to please. I kept saying, "*You can do better. You can do better. You can do better.*" I didn't give the players an indication of how highly I thought of them. Probably I never praised them enough publicly or privately.

'One of my biggest regrets is that I never enjoyed the occasion enough. I was always thinking of the next one. I've learned that if I win anything now I'm going to enjoy it; there's times in life to work and there's times to enjoy. If you achieve something you've got to revel in it, but I was in a hurry to win the next thing. What are we after next?' Only George could have been so calculated and collected. In the midst of the liberating lunacy that enveloped his boys, he marched round like one of Harry Enfield's Scousers urging everyone to calm down. Yet 18 years before, the Stroller had been turning somersaults on the pitch at Wembley as Arsenal beat Liverpool to clinch the Double; funny, that.

Even on the coach back to Highbury, while the euphoric players danced round the back of the bus, drinking as if they had spent the season in the Sahara, George sat at the front with a bottle of champagne in one hand, the Championship silver in the other, and his thoughts in his own head. 'We were thinking, "Surely George has got to let himself go, now of all times," but he didn't,' remembers Rocastle. Back in North London the lads went off to a club appropriately called Winners and the gaffer went home to bed. He got up the next morning aching to get away from it all, and flew to Scotland for a quiet round of golf with his brother and his son. 'I think it all got too much for me,' he reflects.

If it was too intense for the architect to absorb, it had an even deeper effect on the protagonist, Mickey Thomas. In one minute he was transformed from a 21-year-old South London boy who was a gifted professional footballer into a history man. That's what they called him. History Man. Overnight, strangers were falling to their knees in his presence and bowing; others wanted to kiss him (not always a pleasurable sensation where football supporters are concerned); and some men even claimed they wanted to have his babies. Now that can be a terrifying experience for a laid-back dude from Lambeth who is still finding his way in the world. For weeks Arsenal disciples hailed the miracle as part of a daily routine. The competition was on to see who could watch *that* goal most often. Like born-again members of some religious cult, we accosted passers-by and quoted our doctrine: 'It's up for grabs now. George, 19:89. Believe!' The more devoted members of the sect learnt the entire commentary by heart. It took an unreasonable amount of time to return from outer space to the clouds, never mind from the clouds to earth.

Eventually, landing back in North London, it was time to go and collect the winnings from a pre-season bet at odds of 16–1. Beautiful, beautiful life.

When you look back at an old love affair, once the hurt has subsided, your gaze tends to be tinted with a rosy hue. You remember the bliss not the break-up, the multiple orgasms not the bedtime headaches, the Anfields not the Wrexhams. Selective memory again casts its spell. Arsenal want to remember their triumphant times with George Graham for eight years of felicity not two moments of filching. That his transfer record will forever play to the tune of the bung is sadly ironic because – John Jensen, Pal Lydersen and brown envelopes aside – George's moves in the player market embodied the shrewdness of a hustler and the perception of a painter.

George sought players who had the heart and soul, as well as the feet, to play for the Arsenal. 'I wanted to work with committed, passionate people; that was just as important as technique. I looked at the technical ability, the personality, the character, the *desire* [he uses hushed tones to emphasise his favourite trait]. *That lovely word desire.*' Sometimes, George and Ken Friar would meet a potential signing only to be put off the ability because the attitude was lacking. If they felt they had to sell the club to any player, their enthusiasm for the transfer waned; if the cheque was more important than the challenge, the player obviously wasn't right for the club. 'Ken used to say to me, "If he doesn't want to join Arsenal, George, what are we worried about?"'

It's a sign of his immense self-belief that he's not aggrieved if observers gloss over his numerous transfer successes because of two deals arranged by Norwegian agent Rune Hauge which carried the ultimate cost. 'People in football know I'm a good buyer and seller,' he says. In fact, he radiates so much inner confidence he maintains to this day that he never did anything wrong in accepting 'unsolicited gifts' from the over-generous Hauge. The Football Association disagreed, judging £425,000 as a tad too extreme an amount to fall into the 'gift' category. The Graham dynasty was over.

31

Nobody at Highbury wanted George's reign to end shrouded by controversy and bitterness. Not the players: 'I was deeply disappointed,' rues Ian Wright. Not the staff: 'It's terribly sad, he's going to be labelled for the rest of his career when everyone else in football knows that label could be alongside 20 or 30 other people,' reckons Bob Wilson. Not the old boys: 'George was the greatest manager we ever had,' claims Charlie George. Not the fans, who lamented: 'One Georgie Graham' during the match against Nottingham Forest on the day he was sacked. And not the board: 'It was a Greek tragedy, a North London tragedy,' says David Dein. 'We did our very best to understand George's position, or what was ultimately his defence. We really left it to the Football Association and their disciplinary report because they were the fact-finders, the police in the case. When the report came to us we had no alternative but to take the route we did.'

Drama had been a theme running throughout George's time as Arsenal manager, and the epilogue depicts him as the Oedipal figure who manufactured his own downfall. The irony scathed. George Graham, the man who demanded principled behaviour, who preached discipline and correctness, who believed in Arsenal's core values, had sidestepped the rules.

When he joined the club in 1966, the Stroller found it all something of a culture shock, leaving a side full of dandy lads having a lark on the Kings Road for a club with a stiff code of conduct. 'They were always the hierarchy, the establishment club. It was *the* Arsenal, the way *the* Arsenal did things and the way *the* Arsenal expected you to behave.' Perhaps one of the reasons the images of George the disciplinarian, the despotic leader, the Colonel Gadaffi, persisted throughout his reign is because restraint is what he felt the club required of him. He insists he's not really like that. He can be genial and witty and charismatic with the best of them but he didn't feel that was the appropriate public stance. 'Maybe it was the Arsenal way, the dignified way. I believe sometimes the club is too stuffy, too staid, and the same could be said for me. A lot of people thought I was arrogant – I'm not an arrogant person, I'm a little bit difficult to get to know but, once you do, I'm a good friend. Maybe because I'm not as emotional as some would like me to be people mistake that for arrogance. But me getting out the dug-out and waving is not the Arsenal way of doing things. The club is bigger than me, the club is bigger than the team.

'I've never been one for adulation. I've got a good relationship with the Arsenal crowd but I don't think I milked it. I used to enjoy reflected glory if the team won. People would say, "Oh, that George is a clever sod," and that was my buzz. Waving from the dug-out isn't me, I'm too focused on the game. It's weird. Certain managers love it, but I only wanted to be remembered for trophies and success. Looking back I could have been a bit more friendly and relaxed with the fans, but the response I've had since I left the club, I've had lovely letters. When I first went back for Merson's testimonial, it was magnificent. The reception from the fans was really good for me. You cannot believe what that did for me. Maybe the relationship that I thought was reasonably polite was a bit deeper than that. That was important. It went a long way to helping the healing. Basically, everybody likes being liked. I've still got friends within the club, the tea lady, laundry ladies, in the box office, the administration staff, the ground staff – I know them all.'

Is part of you still Arsenal, George? 'Without question there's a little part of me there. How can you spend 15 years at a club and have the success I had without feeling that's part of you? Of course it is. When I'm gone and Arsenal directors are gone, they will remember George Graham.' Like having rose-tinted glasses on, he looks back at his old Arsenal flame and remembers the glory more than the grief.

Woah, I Don't Fancy This

GEORGE ARMSTRONG

Arsenal 3 Anderlecht 0
28 April 1970

Wilson, Storey, McNab, Kelly, McLintock, Simpson, Armstrong,
Sammels, Radford, George, Graham

1966 may have been a great year for English football but for the country's most famous club, managed by the nation's most capped international, Billy Wright, they were the darkest of days. Clouds of doom hovered over Islington and on a wretched Thursday night in May, the heavens opened and poured their wrath over Arsenal. For a rearranged match against Leeds United only 4,554 hardy souls graced the club with their patronage, a record which stands to this day as the lowest attendance at Highbury. It was just as well the proud smile on Herbert Chapman's bust, forever reflecting the glory days of yesteryear, was fixed because he would have worn a thunderous expression. The only other happy faces that night belonged to the men from Yorkshire who eased to a 3–0 victory over an Arsenal side bedraggled in body and spirit. The frustrated few voiced their anguish at the sorry state of the club, aimed primarily at the manager, while the silent majority who stayed away had the consolation of watching Real Madrid win the European Cup live on television. A European final – now wouldn't that be something.

Billy Wright, so the tale goes, was irked by Chapman's lingering presence, and toyed with the idea of ever so accidentally nudging the statue from its pedestal, sending it crashing onto the

Marble Floor. So sorry, chaps. To be reminded of such illustrious traditions every time you walked through the front door only emphasised the inadequacies of the present. There were heated discussions about removing the pictures of Joe Mercer and the Compton brothers with the 1950 FA Cup from the staffroom wall. Ultimately, it was agreed they could only be taken down when there was a picture of a modern player with honours to replace them. Frank McLintock remembers the pressures. 'I was getting Alec Forbes, Alex James, Cliff Bastin and all the greats rammed down my throat quite regularly, with the history of Arsenal people couldn't help it.' Billy Wright, a perfect gentleman, simply didn't have the nerve to drag the club forward. It was time for him to go.

The summer storm set an appropriate scene – Arsenal had hit an equinox, the exact moment when night meets day, when the past hits the future. Four days afterwards, a crowd of 5,123, more than had bothered to turn out to watch the first team, was drawn to Highbury to watch Arsenal win the FA Youth Cup. A glimmer of hope.

Arsenal trainer Bertie Mee was appointed as Wright's replacement. The differences between the two were stark; Wright's playing career was legendary and Mee's was, in generous terms, unremarkable. Wright fell into that euphemistic category of 'too nice to be a manager' whereas Mee, with his army training, was forthright and disciplined. As for the history Wright found burdensome, Mee's views were utterly rational: 'We should be grateful for the past but we cannot live in the past,' he stressed. Only trouble was, people weren't exactly keen on watching 0–3 capitulations at Highbury, and who could blame them for taking the odd day-trip down memory lane? Of the team which surrendered to Leeds, three players survived to play significant roles in Mee's mission: Peter Storey, Jon Sammels and George Armstrong.

First up, the new manager courted the League Cup, but she proved to be a bitterly cruel mistress. Bloody Leeds. Sodding Swindon. Arsenal flirted with success with two dates at Wembley – and that was something after 15 frigid years – only to finish up brokenhearted. As if getting dumped by our friends in the North in the 1968 League Cup Final wasn't miserable enough, the ego was well and truly shattered by Swindon a year later. The capital's bigshots were left crying at the altar while a bunch of bumpkins from the Third Division ran off with the Cup. The indignity of it all was intolerable. Arsenal claimed mitigating circumstances: a flu epidemic had swept through the entire squad bar the Bobs Wilson and McNab, and the pitch was the consistency of sticky manure (a Wembley waterfall drowned a surface already battered by the Horse of the Year show), surely unbefitting Highbury's thoroughbreds. The football world guffawed and hurrahed at these fumbling excuses – it's always a pleasure to see the establishment hauled down a peg or three, and there's an added bonus when it's Arsenal. This is a fact the Gunners must accept; when we triumph praise is grudging and when we fail humiliation is merciless.

In the Wembley dressing-room the lads felt alone in their anguish. Bobby Gould was crying. Peter Simpson chain-smoking. Frank McLintock, who was turning into a football trivia question (which player appeared in four Wembley finals and lost them all?) sat in the bath wallowing in his misfortune until the water was freezing. Nothing like a painfully chastening experience to put things into perspective.

The performance, pilloried in the newspapers as the 'Shame of Arsenal', stiffened Mee's resolve to rescue the season – after all, the team were on course for their best league placing for a decade. 'Our aim,' he claimed stoically, 'is to win a place in the Fairs Cup.' They were prophetic words.

Mee made another speech saturated with resonance about the future after the final game of the campaign at Goodison Park. George Armstrong, one of the senior pros who had been around long enough to play alongside such luminaries as Joe Baker, George Eastham and Jack Kelsey, sensed something was afoot. 'We lost 1–0 at Everton. Really, the performance was pretty poor end-of-the-season stuff. Frank stood up and banged the table, "Bertie, I'd like to say a few words to thank you and Don, we've had a good season, the best for many years . . ." It seemed a lifetime and then Bertie stood up and said, "Okay, Frank, you've started it, now I'll finish it." We all thought *oh-oh*. It was amazing. The little fella banged his fist on the table and said: "Right, that isn't good enough for me. I want to win something and I'm afraid some of you will fall by the wayside. You either turn round and prove people wrong or you'll be gone." He had a lot of pride, did Bertie. I looked at Bob McNab and we thought *blimey.*'

★

1961 was a good year for North London football. Geordie signed for the Gunners. A 17-year-old apprentice electrician and amateur player from the North-East, he jumped on the train to London for a trial expecting nothing, and Arsenal, to be truthful, hardly expected Superman. Such are the vagaries of football. If the little lad was back in Hebburn within the week, he would be perfectly content – 'I wasn't caring whether I stayed or not. I had a good job, was enjoying life and if I failed it wasn't the end of the world' – yet when he left years later, his name was etched in the club's heart as the record appearance holder.

Travelling to London Colney for a trial was the first time Geordie had ever left home. On arrival, reserve coach George Male, one of Herbert Chapman's glory boys of the '30s, asked him his position. Geordie was an inside-forward, 'Oh, we've got plenty of them,' Male interrupted, 'Will you do me a favour and play as a winger?'

'I'll play anywhere you like,' smiled Geordie. And he stayed there for 16 years. What a rise to prominence. He impressed so quickly that in the same month as signing apprenticeship forms, he was back in the manager's office putting pen to a professional contract for the princely sum of £15 a week. He moved in with Vic Groves (uncle of Perry) and six months on he was playing in front of the masses at Highbury.

During the slumber seasons of the '60s, Geordie was probably the most wholehearted performer on Arsenal's books, buzzing up and down those wings as if he was plugged into an electric socket on the touchline. 'I was an honest player and the crowd were great with me because they love a trier,' he says. And try he did, even if some of those around him puffed and sighed as Arsenal plodded through another trophyless season. Geordie just got on with it, running and running without a care like Forrest Gump.

Even after a rigorous cross-country session at training, while his team-mates staggered for the carpark, he took off to pound the miles back home. Fitness fanatic or masochist? 'Running was my second nature,' he explains. Oh.

Geordie threw himself into enjoying his football. 'They were happy times in the '60s,' he recalls. 'We'd win 4–2 or lose 4–3. In that period winning wasn't so important. Some of the football was more enjoyable because there wasn't the pressure there is today. Now it's imperative not to lose, and everyone says "Great result" even if it's been a boring 1–0. We wouldn't accept that in the old days – the game was more fun. The camaraderie was better then and we spent time together when we finished training. Twice a week we trained at Highbury and we all jumped in the big bath whether we was muddy or not and stayed in there about an hour with all the banter. Today, with the modern player, it's shower, mobile phone, agent, gone. I think they've missed out on the laughing and joking and closeness we had. We were mates. But life is different now. We didn't even have an accountant never mind an agent; didn't need one on twenty quid a week.'

They might have had a good crack but there was the small matter of a lack of competitiveness in London N5. Bertie Mee knew that his former role of physiotherapist was both help and hindrance. The upside was his knowledge of the players and the club. And the downside? Occasional digs questioning what a jumped-up physio knows about the finer details of First Division football? To Mee's credit, well aware of his own strengths and weaknesses, he decided to leave the coaching to the coaches rather than busk it at the training ground. His right-hand man was Dave Sexton, a deep thinker whose ideas were all about encouraging the lads to go forward, for which he was immensely popular. While Mee oversaw everything back at Highbury, Sexton had complete control at Colney. McLintock remembers the consequences if the coach had a day off: 'If Dave missed training and Bert tried to take it, he had to pack it in halfway through and give us running. [Good news for Geordie.] He said, "I'm sorry, I can't do it." We found Dave Sexton fantastic and we were so desperate for success we were eating out of his hands. He

38

wanted to leave to be a manager himself and I went to Bertie, "You can't let him go." I remember Bertie's words to this day. "He wants to paddle his own canoe," he said. I thought, "Sod his own canoe! Get him here, because you can't do it. We need someone like that badly! How dare you let him go – the whole team is gutted." He appointed Don Howe as his coach, an ex-player who had broken his leg and was coaching the reserves, and we had trouble at first because we were all sulking and really angry.'

But Sexton was halfway down the Thames and the team had to pull themselves together. 'Oh, the broken hearts on the bus the day it was announced,' remembers Geordie, 'We were going to Wolves that day and we were beaten before we left Southgate.' Final score: Wolves 2 Arsenal 0. Little did the players realise that the man who took up the rudder of the good ship Arsenal would steer them towards greatness. Don Howe was the catalyst for a new chapter of history; the blend between his and Mee's diverse fortes gave Arsenal the inner strength that had been missing for aeons.

Geordie, Don and Frank, who had all played together under Billy Wright, were neighbours living within 40 yards of each other. Overnight, all three had to adapt to the fact that when Don said jump, Geordie and Frank were airbound. Being a relaxed, deferential bloke, Geordie accepted it all in his stride, but Frank, being the opinionated captain, took some winning over. 'One day at Highbury we sussed an atmosphere change,' Geordie recalls. Don called the squad over to clear the air. 'He said, "Right, that's it. From now on, *I'm* in charge and you'll do what *I* tell you. Dave Sexton is gone and I'm here, and now, *we're doing it my way.*" He really laid down the law.

'Don had many strengths. Dave was great with the attacking players but, if you want to win trophies, defence is so important and we didn't have organisation at the back until Don took over. Don was the fire and Bertie was the calm. While Bertie could lose his temper, he didn't have to with Don around. If you did something wrong on the pitch you knew you were going to get it either way. Don didn't miss a thing. He'd give you a little look across the pitch as if to say *I've seen that.* The chemistry was good. If Don was working, good as he was, as soon as the manager came along and stood on the sidelines at Colney, *whoosh*, the training level would rise 5 or 10 per cent – it was respect for the wee man. After a game he would tell you truths but he'd leave it until the following day. He'd say, "We're all fired up, we've all got a bad head. Let's cool down and talk tomorrow." That was a great strength. I've got nothing but admiration for Bertie, a great man manager. He wasn't universally liked but I saw the goodness in the guy. He was the right man at that time, and with Don's backing it was like a jigsaw puzzle coming together.'

About time too. The pain of Highbury's troubled years had been exacerbated by their neighbours' triumphs. Incomprehensible though it might seem to anyone under the age of 35, Arsenal endured a decade living in Tottenham's shadows, which was quite enough, thank you. Geordie had arrived at Highbury while they were celebrating a Double down the Seven Sisters Road, which was followed by three more Cups. When Arsenal bought Tottenham's winger Jimmy Robertson, he brought with him tales of triumph, which made an impression on Geordie: 'We thought we were a good side but I'll always remember Jimmy saying to me, "You'll never *believe* you're a good side until you've won a piece of silverware."'

The last home programme before the Swindon final, yours for just one shilling, took the opportunity to introduce readers to Arsenal's reserve and junior squads. All fresh-faced and clean-cut (that wouldn't last long), there's Charlie George, Ray Kennedy, Eddie Kelly and Sammy Nelson. For some of the club's old stagers, the final was their ninth life; their collapse meant the young cats scratching on the first-team door were let in.

The injection of youth gave Arsenal the shot in the arm which would prove the difference between runners-up and winners. 'The timing was perfect,' Geordie recalls, 'We were getting wiser and the kids came through. The cockney lads had a different attitude, they were more outgoing. Charlie was a one-off, a lot of discipline went out the door the minute he walked in and I mean that in the nicest possible way. I'm not being funny but when we were young if a senior pro walked into the dressing-room we all stood up, and when we were playing table-tennis after training, if a senior player came over you just put the bat down and walked away. You had to.' More chance of Charlie lying flat out on the table than respectfully offering the bat to his elders.

If Geordie was amazed by the cheek of king of the whipper-snappers Charlie George, God knows what the likes of Johan Cruyff made of him. His Ajax team, which boasted six Dutch internationals, could do nothing to stop cocksure Charlie scoring twice in the semi-finals of the Fairs Cup. Not half bad for a teenager in his first season. His fellow débutants, Kennedy and Kelly, would also see their names light up the European stage in 1970.

The Cup run was crammed with variety and spice, a stimulating diversion from the tough English season. 'It was exciting, the smell of the countries was different, the spirit of the stadiums was different, the style of the football was different,' enthuses Bob Wilson. Although the club were seasoned travellers – friendly tours were essential to upholding the good name worldwide – this was only Arsenal's second foray into European competition. Glentoran of Ireland, Sporting Club de Portugal and Rouen of France were brushed aside before a memorable quarter-final tie against the Romanians Dinamo Bacau. Arsenal were greeted by a crowd of thousands at the airport and girls in national costume presented the players with bouquets of flowers. No such welcome for Don Howe and Ken Friar, whose trip had taken them via Zurich and Frankfurt and all sorts as the chairman wouldn't allow them on the Arsenal charter flight. Even before the Munich air disaster, it had always been his policy to take two separate travelling parties, half the players, staff and directors on each, in order to protect the club. The mindboggling cost of hiring two jets for Romania forced a rethink. 'If the plane goes down, at least Ken Friar and Don Howe can rebuild the club again,' considered the chairman. The independent travellers just caught up with the official group in time for the kick-off.

At the stadium Arsenal were cheered onto the field and, after beating the local heroes 2–0, were cheered off it even more vigorously. The trip, never mind the game, was an experience. 'We took a chef and our own food, and when you see how these people live, poverty staring you in the face, it's quite frightening,' remembers Geordie. 'It opens your eyes to the problems of the world. I wouldn't have been there but for football.'

Geordie was on the bench in Romania, his place taken by Peter Marinello. With skills and hairstyle best described as mercurial, he was dubbed the 'Scottish George Best' and his arrival caused Geordie some concern: 'Obviously when the manager buys a new winger you think, "Bloody hell, that's me out the door," but I was a fighter and I thought if he's gonna have it he's gonna have to earn it. Peter had a lot of ability but our lads knew what I could do, they knew I'd be back helping. Peter had things over me but I had things over him which were maybe more important to the team. Anyway, competition is good for anybody. You couldn't play two or three bad games on the trot or you'd be out.' Geordie bustled his way back into the team to face Ajax for the semi-final second leg in Amsterdam. Three goals to the good from the first leg, Arsenal defended like demons to book their first ever European final. Geordie, true to his word, had been back helping. He had to, as the chance to advance was restricted by his opposing full-back, and Siamese twin, Wim Suurbier. 'They talk about man-marking today; well, if you went to the toilet he followed you,' Geordie grins.

One week later Arsenal were back in the Low Countries to face Anderlecht, who stood between them and their first trophy for 17 years. At the Parc Astrid in Brussels, the dazzling Dutchman Jan Mulder succeeded where his Ajax compatriots had failed, and Arsenal's rearguard crumbled to a 3–0 deficit. 'Anderlecht were a great side,' muses Geordie. 'Jan Mulder was probably one of the best centre-forwards I ever saw, absolutely superb. If they had scored six abroad we couldn't have complained because they murdered us.'

Not again, for pity's sake, not again. Yet for the third consecutive season, Mee's men, it seemed, had keeled over at the final hurdle. Having picked themselves up first from the Leeds letdown and then the Swindon soul-searching, this was too much to bear, more of an emotional than sporting battering. It was a wonder Arsenal kept the goals-against down to three; it was a bloody miracle Ray Kennedy, a late substitute, scored with a header before heartbroken Arsenal trudged off the field. Poor Ray. What a unique experience for him – to claim his first goal for the club in what was only his fourth substitute's appearance, and that in a European final – and yet any personal satisfaction he felt was suffocated by the mood of melancholy which enveloped the team.

As for Frank McLintock, he was so low that a dose of Prozac would have brought him up to a state of deep depression. Final number five had knocked him for six.

But the captain's powers of recovery are so potent it would confound every theory of modern psychology. His soul is ruled by spontaneity, and after 15 minutes of self-absorbed silence, he leapt shrieking from the showers in a Eurekan flash, eyes popping like Einstein. '*HEY! GET YOUR FUCKING HEADS UP! WE CAN BEAT THIS TEAM! Have you seen their centre-half, the big fella of six foot two? He cannot head for toffee! In the last ten minutes, with Peter Marinello and Geordie getting crosses in, Ray Kennedy won EVERY SINGLE HEADER! All we need to do is bombard them and WE'LL HAMMER THEM!*' And do you know what? To a man his team-mates believed him. 'By the time we'd left the dressing-room we were going to beat Anderlecht on the home journey,' chuckles Frank. So, Kennedy got his pats on the back after all.

No one dared to remind the skipper that Arsenal's only previous appearance in European competition, some five years before, had ended with a 3–1 defeat in Belgium at the hands of FC Liege.

28 April. Anderlecht at home. The date Frank McLintock will either be hailed an inspired soothsayer or a total crackpot. Highbury has been preparing for this date with destiny since dawn. All day the staff have gone about their business with rosettes pinned to their clothes, their eyes counting down with the clocks and their heads drifting into fantasy land. 'We're all fans too, you know,' nods Ken Friar.

The fans flock to Highbury full of anticipation and, like the players, stick their chests out and believe. Arsenal need to score twice to win on away goals and, so far in Europe, the boys have bagged three at Highbury against Glentoran, Sporting and Ajax, and seven against Bacau. So why not? Of course there is the small matter of containing Jan Mulder and co, but bravado is the order of the day. The message 'Come on, Gunners – shoot to kill' is plastered over every billboard in N5. The crowd prepare their tonsils to put three seasons' worth of pent-up hurt into 90 minutes. The grand old stadium shakes with excitement.

The players, as is routine, meet up at South Herts golf course for their pre-match meal, then relax with a game of snooker or a putt or two on the green. Then the team-talk, Bertie Mee, up-right as ever, plays the mind games while Don Howe, pacing and pointing, gets stuck into tactics. For all the rampaging attacks, keeping the Belgians at bay was equally vital.

On to Highbury. Geordie can't believe his eyes: 'The atmos-phere was the best I've ever seen, absolutely incredible. There was a full house of 52,000 and there must have been about 40,000 outside that couldn't get in – the streets were full. It was some-thing unique and magical. They talk about the fervent support in the North . . . that night just showed you how North London could get behind their team with the best of them. The terraces were packed, like our 12th man. Anderlecht really thought it was all over but we thought, "Here we are, the underdogs with nothing to lose," and one thing the team was capable of was scrapping. We all found energy that night, we dug down deep in our boots and found extra. Every factor came together that night. It rained here and we watered the pitch and then did a bit more watering [he winks]. I remember their faces, you could see them thinking "*Woah, I don't fancy this.*" We had one up on them from the start.'

It's one up for real ten minutes before half-time, as Eddie Kelly carves an opening on the edge of the area and drives the ball past Jean Trappeniers for only his second Arsenal goal. The frenzied roar of approval shudders through the night sky. The players' conviction, which was already total, goes into overload. 'Once Eddie scored we knew they couldn't stand the pressure,' says Geordie. 'Psychologically we had turned the corner and we sensed we would win. The guy I was playing against, Heylens, I could see it in his face, *Cor blimey.* It was a red flag to a bull. *Here we go, we can win this!* There was great belief. Now we're on our way. I never felt tired that night. I felt as if I could run on and on and on and on. The adrenaline was so high that when it came to digging in and fighting, they weren't going to beat us.'

Into the second half and the relentless din rolls round the ground like an aural Mexican wave. *Attack! Attack! Attack attack attack!* Geordie, who by his own admission froze in the Wembley finals, is red hot at Highbury, launching ball after ball into the Anderlecht goalmouth and each one strikes a blow to Belgian resolve. Then Bob McNab pelts forward, plants a cross onto John Radford's head, it's 2–0 and the place goes mental. Before High-bury has a chance to catch its breath, Jon Sammels shimmies past his man, slams the ball into the net . . . and a 17-year-old detona-tor goes off. Sammy, Raddy and Geordie wail *YEEAARRGGHH!* at 20,000 wild faces in the North Bank and we all wail *YEEAARRGGHH!* back. Sometimes in life you don't need to find words. Only utterly unintelligible noise can express what you really feel.

Geordie reckons it was in the stars all along. 'It was fate. For 15 minutes after the third goal we couldn't give a goal away, which flashed across my mind even though I was sure we had it won. They hit the post, but it was too late for them. I'm a fatalist and I believe some things in life are meant to happen. I mean, who the hell knows when you bring a sub on if he's going to turn the game for you, like Ray did in Belgium? We were due one. And that was it.'

Somewhere in amongst the cacophony of celebration the referee's whistle signals the end of the match and the beginning of an almighty knees-up on the pitch. In rare moments of pure emotion such as these, people find a talent they didn't know they had; the ability to weep, beam, bearhug, dance and fall to the ground in giddy gratitude, all at the same time, which is quite something.

Back in the dressing-room, big Frank McLintock, a winner at last, is crying; wee Geordie, the longest-serving player in the team, has finally stopped running and is for once shattered; Charlie George, who would have been in the North Bank if he wasn't on the pitch, is being manhandled by Don Howe; John Radford – 'one of the best centre-forwards this country has ever seen', according to Geordie – has his head in the clouds; Peter Simpson, so classy at the back, takes a deep, deep drag on his cigarette.

The board of directors come down to congratulate the lads and feast their eyes on the enormous piece of silver. It's a marvellous moment for Denis Hill-Wood, who genuinely adores the players and the feeling, says Geordie, is mutual. 'One of the factors was winning it for him, the old chairman was magic. He was the best ever, a superb, special guy; he was a gentleman, a scholar and, sink or swim, he and the group of directors would come down. Even if we lost he would console us, *Never mind, boys.* Winning wasn't everything to him – he loved the club and was proud of the reputation. And he was so pleased. It was one hell of an achievement.'

Don Howe believes the Cup was the board's reward for keeping faith after the traumas of Swindon: 'It would have been easy for the directors to panic and maybe get rid of me and Bertie but they never stopped backing us and they were repaid for that.' Ironically, two years before, Hill-Wood had gone on record expressing his Euroscepticism, suggesting Arsenal might gratefully decline the invitation to play in the Fairs Cup if they qualified. Thank goodness he didn't back his judgement that time.

Some time afterwards, Geordie saw his old pal Jimmy Robertson who had moved on to Ipswich. He remembered his maxim about a club needing to win a cup before they could believe in themselves. 'Bloody hell,' exclaimed Robertson, 'now you *are* a good side.' It was the springboard which enabled the team to leap to even loftier peaks. 'Anderlecht was so important for the club and all of a sudden the expectations grew,' remembers Geordie. 'For the younger players the experience of winning a trophy gave them the confidence to go on to the Double. It happens that a team comes together for some reason. They have talent but it's the camaraderie and honesty that makes them a very good side. I think it was always there but we just needed something to light the blue touchpaper. The Fairs Cup did it.' The albatross of history had been slayed. Now Arsenal could fly to greater heights.

My Shout

FRANK McLINTOCK

Tottenham 0 Arsenal 1
3 May 1971

*Wilson, Rice, McNab, Kelly, McLintock, Simpson, Armstrong,
Graham, Radford, Kennedy, George*

It's an accepted medical theory that bottling up your emotions can make you ill. Let your feelings fester away for too long inside your head and your body eventually finds a way of saying 'enough'. That's probably the reason why most of us go to football in the first place, as it's the one area in our lives where people, men particularly, can express the spectrum of human reaction without fear of humiliation. Outside the sanctuary of the game, we wouldn't dream of walking down the street singing about who we loved, or leaping into the arms of a stranger, or accusing a passer-by of being a visually challenged illegitimate masturbator. Well, words to that effect. Not unless we'd downed a crate of Special Brew, anyway.

But through football we can let it all out – from angst to *amour*, from loathing to lunacy – safe in the knowledge that nobody will mock us or lock us up for it. Nobody could care less, partly because everyone is too busy releasing their own tensions to worry about anyone else's cranky behaviour, partly because everyone is obsessed by the team and, most importantly, because everyone is in it together. The whole point about teamwork is that a common aim makes personal differences or conflicting quirks melt away.

47

Take, for example, John Radford and Bob Wilson, two crucial cogs in the Double machine. Radford was a tough nut when he turned up at Highbury, brought up in a Yorkshire pit village where spades were your bloody bare hands when he were a lad. Wilson, however, waltzed into London in his dashing Austin Healey Sprite, sporting his college scarf and dufflecoat. Stick them next to each other in a hospital waiting-room and they would presumably find it easier to read a constipation leaflet than strike up a conversation, but throw them both in the same team and they'd fight for each other until they were out cold. 'With a footballer it doesn't matter if one was born Little Lord Fauntleroy and one was born down a mine,' claims Wilson. 'At the end of the day a footballer has only one question he wants answering: *Can he play?* Do I think John Radford can play? Yes. Does he think I can play? Yes. Raddy thought I was the best goalkeeper in the whole of England and I thought he was the best centre-forward. That is the bread and butter of football; you may be worlds apart but you're *together*.' As it turned out, they grew to become great friends.

Take George Armstrong and Peter Simpson, who roomed together, which was akin to Mr Motivator waking up with Fag Ash Lil; while Geordie was a fitness freak, Peter sucked so hard on his cigarettes the smoke would end up in his toenails, and that after a pint of brandy and coke on a Saturday night. While Geordie was happy-go-lucky incarnate, Peter earned the nick-name Stan, after Stan Laurel, for his deadpan expression. Yet they became inseparable. The players on the pitch, odd hotchpotch of characters as they were, all craved the same thing, and each individual appreciated the others' virtues.

Nat Lofthouse used to say when you kick one man you kick 11 men. That was the philosophy which underpinned the Arsenal team of 1970–71. It was a concept the captain Frank McLintock actively encouraged, to ensure the team spirit was 100 per cent proof. Before long, even the teetotals in the squad were intoxicated. If the lads went out for a drink they went mob handed, not splintered into bitty groups. If there was a do on, Frank would announce 'We're all going!' and woe betide anyone who didn't fancy it. Once Bob Wilson had the temerity to explain that

48

he didn't drink. Frank, never one to store his emotions for more than two seconds, was having none of it. '*I don't care if you don't drink! Give us your fiver, that's going in the whip – you can drink 40 bottles of Coca-Cola if you want. We're going somewhere, we're going TOGETHER!*' Thus was born a team ethic more powerful than a juggernaut. Leeds? Tottenham? Liverpool? Get out of the way.

Spirit was further fortified by a dash of foreign spice when Arsenal visited Rome for round one of the Fairs Cup defence against Lazio. Round two took place with fists instead of feet in the Italian streets a few hours after the game. It had been a brutal contest at the Stadio Olimpico and tempers were still simmering in the post-match soirée held at a swanky restaurant. Entertaining both teams at the same venue probably wasn't the smartest idea, considering the scything tackles which had marked the occasion, the worst of which almost snapped George Armstrong in two. Peter Storey, the embodiment of all 11 men feeling one man's assault, was in unforgiving mood. He spent the entire meal scowling at the Italians. As Frank remembers, it set the tone: 'Peter was growling all night and we says to him, "For Christ sake, Snouty, sit down." He was always growling, anyway – even on the pitch he would growl, letting the guy he was marking hear him *gggrrrr* and I used to think I'm glad he's playing for me, not against me. He made a lot of noise on the pitch and I'm sure it frightened a lot of players.

'Ray Kennedy went out for a breath of fresh air, and their captain and a couple of supporters walked by and said something to him, and Ray, who wouldn't take any lip from anyone, gave some back and they started fighting. Then Peter Marinello went out and he was getting thrown across a car by these supporters. And then Bob Wilson ran out and ran straight back in saying [Frank affects a jelly-like voice], "*There's a fight outside . . .*" So me and Eddie Kelly, who liked a fight, we were out there. It went off for about ten minutes, there was someone on my back punching the back of my head and I had hold of his pal whacking him. All of a sudden the police came and pulled their guns out.' End of skirmish. The moral of the story is anytime, anyplace, anywhere. Which doesn't refer to a liking for a flurry of fisticuffs, but does affirm that every Arsenal man could rely, absolutely, on the help of his team-mates. And they didn't even have to be asked.

The second moral of the story is that Bertie Mee ordered the players to stay inside the hotel in an attempt to keep the indiscretion as minor as possible, but Frank and George Graham, unable to resist the swish party they had been invited to, sneaked out the back door and into the sumptuous night. 'This was George's idea of discipline,' laughs Frank, whereby hangs another tale.

When the team landed back in England, they were greeted from the plane by a ravenous media, eager to feed on another 'shame of football' feast. As ever, it served only to solidify the bond within the team, and as far as they were concerned, they had a way of sorting things out for themselves and it was nobody else's business. If a mate was set upon you wouldn't be much of a friend if you left him to it. And Arsenal were pals. Sometimes, travelling to away matches, Frank would look around the bus checking on his team-mates one by one: 'I'd think, "Yep, yep, yep, no problem." You knew, if you were up against it, you could count on every one of them.'

Frank's love for team spirit was infectious. Being a born enthusiast and a man who doesn't require a telescope to aim for the stars, he wanted the Arsenal unity to be the strongest football would ever see. Don Howe is unequivocal about the impact he made: 'You could put a lot of Arsenal's success in that period down to Frank. He created this *we'll win this together* mentality. Frank was an outstanding captain, a wonderful leader of men, a wonderful presence in the dressing-room.' His quest for glory nagged him with the overwhelming intensity of a drug addict aching for a hit, and he searched, relentlessly, for ways to satisfy the craving. Howe lived next door but one from Frank and every day they drove to and from Highbury together, thrashing out methods to get the best out of the team. 'He'd stamp off into his house and I'd stamp off into mine and the next morning we'd start all over again,' smiles Howe.

The coach was used to having deep discussions about the game. It was an era when Howe, together with the likes of Bobby Robson and Malcolm Allison, spent endless hours after matches analysing football over cups of tea. What made Arsenal so special was that the players did the same. Frank's extraordinary passion for success was mirrored in his team-mates, and Bob McNab, Jon Sammels and John Radford were equally deep thinkers about the game.

Crucially, they didn't just theorise, they acted. If you walk down the players' tunnel at Highbury, at the midway point there is a small door which leads into a room known inside the club as the halfway house. Inside, there are a few tables and chairs and a huge swivelling blackboard, the setting for the Arsenal think-tank, and here, the most highly charged scenes outside the perimeter of the pitch took place. Monday team meetings were no-holds-barred verbal batterings, with Frank acting as referee. Bertie Mee struck the first blow, then Don Howe, then the captain, then all the players charged into a general free-for-all. 'It was all finger-pointing and no hesitation,' Frank reminisces. 'We grew up in an environment where if you did wrong you got bloody told. There was no screwing your way out of it, you had to take it on the chin and make sure you didn't dare do it again. If we got beat we always rebounded well, because the team would be furious – oh the shouting and bawling going on . . .' McLintock, a combination of Marje Proops and a sergeant-major, coaxed the boys into releasing their feelings. He sub-scribed to the view that suppressing your emotions is unhealthy, and, after venting forth, Arsenal always emerged in fine fettle.

Stoke City 5 Arsenal 0. After an upbeat start to the 1970–71 season came the bombshell. If some bright spark had set a camera rolling in the halfway house the following Monday it would have been a blockbuster. The response? Arsenal 4 Notting-ham Forest 0.

If a particularly sensitive matter arose, Frank had a little routine to save tempers from combusting: 'I used Don Howe sometimes. I used to say to him: "Steam into me in this team meeting. I'll argue back but you'll get your points in that you want to make, and using me as a vehicle, you can hammer a point to Charlie or John Radford." If *I* took it, the others *had* to take it.' The positive thing about these slanging matches was that it never deteriorated into the delicate realms of the personal.

What was said in the halfway house was accepted, and used, for the benefit of the team, and when they shut the door behind them the lads would all go off for a drink and toast morale. Don Howe, who has seen it all at club and international level, never witnessed team spirit like it before or since: 'The Double team were special as a group of men because not only did they have this terrific will to win but they could also accept criticism. They had some ding-dongs but the great thing about it was their reaction, a man's reaction. *I'll show you. The things you said I couldn't do this morning? I'll show you I CAN do them.*' Arsenal thought hard, shouted hard and partied hard. And they trained hard. Powerful stuff for a Monday morning.

★

An alien landing at Highbury during 1971 would be forgiven for thinking the creature wearing a red-and-white number 5 jersey was called a Frank-McLintock-inspirational-captain, so regularly were the last two words suffixed to the first pair. Therefore it's frightening to think that Frank's leadership qualities were almost lost to Arsenal before that fateful year. Having joined the club for a record fee of £80,000, and tried his darnedest to justify that, he came close to abandoning ship with a transfer request after the indignity of losing to Swindon. Arsenal were not what he was led to expect for the following reasons: one, Billy Wright had indicated internationals Gordon Banks, Ray Wilson and Don Howe were Highbury-bound yet two never came, one had to quit through injury, and the squad remained sketchy; two, Frank had more ambition in his sleep than the rest of the club on a Saturday; three, he was damned if he was going to waste his career grafting away in Arsenal's midfield, speeding from box to box for a team stuck in neutral.

Then came the masterstroke which invigorated player and club. Typical of Arsenal, the defence was the key to unlock the future. Frank took a step backwards to move forwards. When Don Howe mentioned in one of their noisy car journeys that he'd make a fine centre-back, Frank scoffed. 'I got the hump,' he confesses, less than inspired at the prospect. 'You'll see,' whistled Howe knowingly, and within weeks the coach's instincts were confirmed by Arsenal's born-again defender, wearing his new mantle with refreshing relish.

It was Howe's first move in a game of tactical chess which saw powerless pawns replaced by bishops, knights and kings across the board: Peter Simpson also slipped from midfield to defence, allowing his cool awareness, clean tackling and cultured distribution to flourish; Peter Storey, with his commanding ability and attitude, became a dependable midfield anchorman, leaving the right-back spot free for a determined Pat Rice; George Graham's urbane talents blossomed when he withdrew into midfield, which allowed Ray Kennedy to strike up a happy marriage with John Radford in attack. Checkmate. After months of plotting, the winning formula clicked into place.

'When Ray Kennedy came in and joined up with John Radford, it was made in heaven,' remembers Frank. 'George Graham had been playing with John and they didn't work so well, Raddy used to complain, "This lazy bastard, I've got to do the hard work for him," and George would just raise his eyebrows. When Ray came on the scene they hit it off immediately. Both of them would run all day, both would get up and flick balls on for each other, hold the ball up, lay it off, make runs.' Radford took Kennedy on as his protégé, guiding him through the season on the field and watching out for him off it; often inviting him round to the family home for lunch after training and feeding him nuggets of advice as a room-mate on away trips. Frank reckons it worked a treat. 'When Ray Kennedy came in we all thought, *bloody hell.* He had an assurance about him right from day one. He could ping the ball without any backlift, a very accurate shooter of the ball with great balance. He should have got lots of penalties the way people rattled into him but he never went over. He just rocked a little then stayed on his feet.

'Then with George settling into midfield, he found a new lease of life as well. He was always a graceful passer of the ball with a good eye for the game and his heading was excellent. Being a midfield player at six foot, he came in late and scored some great goals. Peter Storey was a very astute player, he knew how to close people down and very seldom gave the ball away or got caught out of position. He was obviously a little bit vicious

53

at times, if you said to him: "Snouty, get on Eusebio and do him right away. Get into him and tackle him as many times as you can!", he would do it.

'Defensively we were ahead of our time, as former midfield players both Peter Simpson and I were comfortable running into the heart of the opposition midfield. We had the shortest back four in the football league, probably in the history of the football league, so we had to be good at tactics. Simmo was one of the nicest, most unassuming guys you could meet, but if you listened to him off the field you'd cut your throat. He was the biggest pessimist under the sun. When we played Wolves Derek Dougan deliberately came in to see us before the game and he used to look ten feet tall, trying to scare us. As soon as he would leave, Peter used to say, "You pick him up at corner-kicks, Frank." I would say, "Bollocks, I'll pick him up when he's on my side, you pick him up when he's on your side. You're the same size as me." Then Franny Lee would come down with Man City and Peter would mutter, "Franny Lee's too quick for us." You had to tell him to shut up: "Stan, shut your effin' mouth, just get on the pitch!" And once he crossed that line he was absolutely superb, he'd tackle clean as a whistle and weave his way past people like it was easy.

'When I went back to centre-half I seemed to get a new status again and a better understanding of the game. I was more assured at the back, I felt more in control of myself and I could see the bigger picture. Don Howe and Bob McNab helped me a lot when it came to defensive tactics. Little Bob especially – he was very tuned in. If I even moved five yards the wrong way I would get a right bollocking from Bob, "*Get over here! You're affecting my position!*" I learned very quickly. Moving to the back I got a better all-round view of the game, which made me better at giving advice.'

Frank's new confidence in defence was symbolised by the crescendo of sound which accompanied his game. While half of his energy was driven into his feet, the other half fuelled his mouth. The veins in his neck worked as much overtime as the muscles in his thighs, exhorting instructions, encouragement and rollockings from first whistle to last of every game. Although

Frank was chief chorister, there were vibrant vocalists throughout the side. If the enemy was weak, intimidation was an added bonus and, as they howled at each other, Frank occasionally glimpsed an opponent's brow furrowing, utterly bewildered, metaphorically ducking as these deafening volleys whistled past. If Arsenal sensed a striker's nerve had snapped, they would go for the kill. '*Let him run, he's miles offside,*' bawled the back four, even if their tight trap had been breached. Said forward more often than not duly gave up the chase. Very cunning.

Arsenal were the masters of tactical shouting, particularly in defence. McLintock, McNab and Wilson were three men who read the game out loud – extremely loud. Just as well they did, because Pat Rice needed nursing through his first full season and John Roberts, who deputised for the injured Peter Simpson as the campaign got under way, was a nervous player. Having suffered a cruciate ligament injury he was always a tad tentative when he stepped into the fray, and as soon as he received a knock he tumbled to the turf full of worried agony. These were the days before multiple substitutes and his fellow defenders weren't going to let him leave the field unless he needed an ambulance. Remembers Wilson: 'Frank, Bob and myself would stand over the top of him screaming abuse at this huge Welshman: "*GET UP, YOU COWARD!*" And he'd pick himself up, angry at being accused of cowardice, and off he'd go. He was tremendous from then on.'

In a game against Wolves, Rice incurred the wrath of Frank and was almost ambulance-bound as a result. Says McLintock: 'I grabbed Pat round the throat and rammed his head against a post because he backheeled the ball in the six-yard box and subsequently Derek Dougan nearly kicked Bob Wilson's head off. I got hold of him and said, "*Don't you ever try backheels like that! Your best ball is 40 yards up the pitch. That's your strength, defending and clearing your lines, not trying fancy tricks in your own box!*" We would really have a go at each other in a big way.'

It was all born out of an innate hatred of losing. Out on the pitch in front of 55,000, the lads were unscrupulous; if anyone deserved an earbashing they'd get it, and they'd take it because the team came first. They were so pumped up scenes in the dressing-room rendered the halfway house chats decidedly coy – earplugs and mouthguards should have been handed out on the door to anyone who had underperformed. Wilson reckons Frank charged into it like a one-man Highland Light Infantry. Friendships went out the window for that forceful 15 minutes, and the skipper had no scruples about creating merry hell, even for his best mate and partner in crime, George Graham: 'He and I nearly had 200 punch-ups at half-time with me diving at him as soon as he walked through the door, shouting, *"You left your man! And I'm caught between your man and my man! You pick him up!"* He kept his head down unless I was going to hit him or something. We were really fiery at half-time, we would tear at each other, nearly have a fight if one goal went in against us. It meant that much to us. We would be at each other's throats but we were honest because we felt it was so important to make sure we got it right for the second half. There was that winning mentality which all stemmed from a desperation to become winners ourselves. We were a group of really dedicated guys. That's not to say we didn't enjoy ourselves – we certainly did, more than most in fact – but we were also deeply into football. And we loved it.'

Arsenal's motto, *victoria concordia crescit* – victory through harmony, was strangely appropriate. Theirs was a modern interpretation, a bold, brash symphony which swirled through discordant tension and melodic resolution on the way to a rousing finale. The orchestra performed it with gusto.

No one wants to be a one-hit wonder. After the thrill of Anderlecht, Arsenal yearned for the heady sensation of triumph again. By March 1971 they were hurtling full pelt towards whatever they could get their hands on. Second in the league and down to the last four of the FA Cup, the Gunners turned their attentions to the Fairs Cup quarter-final and a trip to Cologne.

With self-belief soaring, the team had no qualms about protecting a 2–1 advantage created at Highbury in the first leg. It soon developed into a melodramatic game wracked, and wrecked, by dark controversy. The antics of Romanian referee Constantin Petres rendered Arsenal almost speechless. As if punishing their customary hollering wasn't bad enough, he awarded a penalty which never was. McNab was tripped up in his own box, a Cologne striker fell on top of him, Petres pointed to the spot, Arsenal lost 1–0 and relinquished their grasp on the trophy on away goals. Frank still seethes about it. 'Every time we called for the ball, "*Raddy hold onto it!*" he blew his whistle and gave a free-kick against us. I tried to explain: "Referee, we're shouting to our own players!" but he simply waved his arms about and flashed yellow cards. And as for the penalty, it was a disgrace. The referee was a nightmare.'

Treble hopes trashed, Arsenal couldn't afford to brood with an FA Cup semi-final only four days away, immediately followed by a gruelling run of eight league games in three weeks. The lads needed to refocus so they resorted to that tried and tested method, a hard talking session. For once, the players listened rather than leapt in. Sensing that the Double teetered on the edge of a precipice, Bertie Mee addressed the squad, voice quivering, loaded with gravitas. Bob Wilson remembers his words. 'He had us all in the dressing-room and said, "I want you now to put football and this club before your families. I want you now to dedicate yourselves because you have a chance to put yourselves in the record books. We're talking about two months of your lives, at the end of which you might have won one, you might have won nothing . . . But you could win both. We *can* march on in the Cup. We *can* catch Leeds."' It was a defining moment. The players usually listened more attentively to Howe, whom they trusted on the minutiae of football, while Mee impressed the importance of the grander issues. This time his message, pregnant with meaning, washed over all of them. The Double was on.

Outside N5 they would have chortled. Apart from the fact the Double had only been achieved once during the 20th century – and that by a team with more fabled flamboyance than anyone would dream of attributing to Arsenal – Leeds were clear favourites for the title. But their six-point advantage was deceptive as Mee's men had three games in hand, and what no bookie calculated was the probability of Arsenal amassing an astonishing 23 points from their last 26. Such sheer resilience was startling. 'There was some pressure on us but we were a very difficult team to beat. I know it sounds ridiculous, but if either us or Leeds were playing today, we'd win the Championship,' declares Frank.

'Leeds United were, for me, probably the best team in the '70s. They had 16 internationals in their squad and should have won so much. Bremner and Giles and Hunter and Lorimer — what a midfield that was. Allan Clarke was a great England centre-forward, and Mick Jones and Jackie Charlton . . . but they were also a very dirty team, up to every trick under the sun.' At half-time in a bruising encounter with Leeds, Don Howe yelled that if he didn't know Frank better he'd think he was a coward, a remark McLintock baulked at. Holding back from a confrontation against them was simply a matter of self-preservation. 'It wasn't to do with being afraid – you were worried you might get a broken leg. You never knew with certain players in the Leeds team if they were going to go in over the top. They were a great side but they knew how to dish it out.'

By the time the two most physically and mentally titanic teams of their era collided at Elland Road, the end of the season was nigh. Arsenal had clambered their way to the top of the table and arrived in Yorkshire with a point, and a game in hand, over Leeds. The searing tension erupted in the devastating, dying moments of conflict when Charlton, with every Arsenal man convinced he was offside, slid the ball past Wilson. 'We went potty,' cries Frank, yet four minutes of vigorous protestations yielded nothing but criticism from Arsenal's detractors. Leeds, with one match left to play, had clawed their way back in front. The following Saturday they duly secured their final two points, with Highbury witnessing a victory the same afternoon. All that remained of the league programme was Arsenal's climactic game in hand. That extra fixture pitted Arsenal against, of all teams, Tottenham. Bertie Mee's words which had inspired such a compelling run still resonated. *You might win one, you might win nothing . . . but you could win both.* Arsenal woke up on Sunday morning, nursing tired legs and trembling souls, two games away from the Double. White Hart Lane tomorrow, Wembley Saturday. *You could win both.*

3 May. Tottenham away. North London is in a state of apo-
plexy. Well over 100,000 fans descend on White Hart Lane,
bunking off school, nicking off from work, desperate to see this
most momentous of matches. The derby in these parts is always
a painfully intense experience, and this is a derby reverberating
with additional agonies – being the last day of the season it
becomes torture; with the Championship at stake it becomes
barbaric; hurl the Double onto the fire and it becomes a
kamikaze religious crusade.

The scene is set: Arsenal can collect part one of a possible
Double at the home of their bitterest foes. Not only that, the
enemy also happen to value it as a very personal possession. In
1961 Tottenham became the only team in living memory to have
managed the feat (it's necessary to return to the nineteenth
century to find the previous winners Preston and Aston Villa)
and they would sooner write *Boring, boring Tottenham* a thousand times than let the Gunners win. 'Arsenal have got as much
chance of being handed the title by Spurs as I have of being given
the crown jewels,' exclaimed their captain Alan Mullery. Incidentally, Tottenham required victory to guarantee a place in
Europe. And some people in Leeds thought North London might
get all cliquey and one club would gift the league to the other.
And the Pope's going to deflower mother superior. 'GO! GO!
GUNNERS!' claimed the front page of the *Evening News.*
Tottenham must have been thrilled with that.

As if there wasn't enough edge to the occasion, mathematical
complexities spike the drama. With Arsenal a point behind
Leeds, a win either way would be conclusive, but a tie would
mean the title decided by goal averages – nil-nil would give
Arsenal the trophy but any scoring draw would hand Leeds the
Championship. Frank is as psyched-up as he's ever been. 'The
build-up was fantastic. There was a feeling of quiet self-con-
fidence. *We'll do this lot, and at their ground as well.* I've never seen
so many people outside a ground except maybe at Wembley. Our
bus crawled along the White Hart Lane for ages and I spotted my
wife in this heaving mob on the pavement. I stopped the bus and
dragged her on. Bertie Mee got the hump with me and I did with
him – as if I was going to leave my wife in that. They had been

queuing since 12 o'clock. I've met people who arrived then and never got in, and they name that as the biggest disappointment in their whole life.'

The fortunate 51,192 fanatics inside the ground make such a clamour that Arsenal's vociferous players can barely hear themselves think, let alone make out the cannonades of encouragement they aim at each other. Even more amazing is that after every roar, every song, comes the echo from the similar number outside. The football is understandably frantic, scurrying and hurrying inexorably to the 0–0 draw which would herald Arsenal's record eighth title. Inside the last ten minutes the ball falls to Frank in the Tottenham box. 'I was just going in to lump it, and the ball hit the referee Kevin Howley, loosened his front tooth and he fell back on his arse. I called him every name imaginable – I didn't care about his tooth. I was going to make a name for myself, ram the ball in the net and he got in the way! And it knocked him flying!' With three minutes left on the clock it is Tottenham who are knocked flying. The ubiquitous Armstrong chases his most vital lost cause of the season and delivers his most telling cross, Kennedy leaps and hangs in the air while the crowd gasps for breath, then floats a divinely arced header over Pat Jennings and in off the bar. Heavenly.

Frank and the boys at the back try desperately hard to stay down on earth, as Tottenham scamper immediately into the Arsenal box. Surprisingly enough, in order to survive the on-slaught, the Gunners resort to the habit of the season. 'We were just shouting at each other: *Get in!* and *Get up!* and *Head it!* and *Whack him!* All I was thinking about was to keep slogging, keep faith.' Poor Bob Wilson is on the receiving end of a Tottenham kickboxing exhibition, and one of Mullery's moves slices his ear open. Frank is livid. 'Alan was really wound up, more so than I've ever seen him. How he wasn't sent off, I'll never know. He and Alan Gilzean kept on rattling Bob about the head. We wanted to get retribution, oh aye, bang them and punch them, but we had to be careful, we knew if one of us got sent off they might beat us. We could understand to an extent why they were doing it – we would have done the same. It's an emotional game, football. We wanted to chin them, but once the goal went in we just had to keep nice and calm, be resolute, talk to each other.

'We were so used to being bombarded. People thought we were lucky yet we knew exactly what we were doing. We knew how to defend and we trusted each other implicitly. It was going to take something extraordinary to beat us that night. Mind you, it seemed ages before we actually heard that final whistle.' When Howley purses lips to whistle for the last time, the green of the White Hart Lane grass is transformed into a blur of red-and-white jubilation as half the ground cascades towards their heroes. 'The fans nearly strangled me,' says Frank, still alive to tell the tale, 'so many thousands on the pitch and everyone wants a bit of you. I was up on somebody's shoulders and they all threw scarves round my neck. They all wanted to pat me. I'm not kidding you, I was exhausted. When people pull you all different ways, and it lasts for about 20 minutes, you get a bit panicky. I thought I would get suffocated, they were that frenzied. I was dying to get back into the dressing-room to see my team-mates because we were all separated for about half an hour. We just wanted to grab each other, fantastic, all that training, all that hard work, all that running through ploughed fields. And then the reward. I loved that night. It was everything I wanted. Winning the Championship at last and just bursting with love for your fellow players. All you want to do is get together with them and share the feelings. All those hard games, and all of it came right. What a feeling that was.' To Tottenham's credit, they delivered bottles of bubbly to the Arsenal dressing-room. Some of them even wished the boys good luck for Saturday.

Bertie Mee, a man who prided himself on his formal behaviour, lost himself in the passion of it all. Jacket off – in itself a surprising event – he hugged his players warmly, another rarity. Usually it was Don Howe who was the physical presence in the dressing-room, he was the one who grabbed hold of the lads while Mee remained discreet and at a distance. The crowd called for Bertie, flatly refusing to leave until he made an appearance, and he abandoned his usual restraint by emerging in the directors' box, relaxed in his shirt-sleeves, to greet the fans. He returned, a little shaken by hundreds of demented backslappings and embraces. 'Their joy even outjoyed England's World Cup

Victory,' eulogised the *Daily Express*. And the celebrations went on all week, merging into the excited build-up to the Cup Final. Mee, in another act of uncharacteristic insouciance with five days till Wembley, granted his players the night off to rejoice to the full. Frank went to the pub in Southgate to cherish the moment until five o'clock in the morning.

Our Darling

CHARLIE GEORGE

Arsenal 2 Liverpool 1 (aet)
8 May 1971

Wilson, Rice, McNab, Storey, McLintock, Simpson, Armstrong,
Graham, Radford, Kennedy, George

Charlie George always was something of an enigma. How else do you begin to explain his movements after that Championship-winning night at White Hart Lane? Charlie, the quintessential Arsenal man, born in Islington and bred on the North Bank, having just played in the most liberating derby any Gooner could ever witness . . . what did he do when the team coach drew up at Southgate? He hopped on the tube and went home. The lads hit the boozer, his old man and fiancée were out looking for him to help their favourite boy paint the town red and white. And Charlie went home. He just felt like it, so he did.

Like I say, enigmatic. Little wonder moody pubescents all over London wished they could be like Charlie George. And frivolous nymphettes wished they could be with Charlie George. And bashful housewives wished they could mother Charlie George. And that's before even mentioning what Charlie meant to the Arsenal faithful. He was one of us, and he was living out all of our fantasies.

In the judgemental eyes of the fan there are seven deadly sins unforgivable in a footballer: greed (bloody mercenary), sloth (lazy sod), gluttony (Fatboy), wrath (unnecessary red card and FA disrepute charge), jealousy (whingeing in the papers), lust (maybe that's not so unforgivable considering most supporters wouldn't object to having groupies) and pride. The most indefensible crime of all, pride, a player who doesn't try. Logic tells me that no player actually has a stinker on purpose, but from the irrational vantage-point of the stands, someone having a bad day at the Highbury office is an infuriating sight. The reaction from the masses is always the same. Thousands of hopelessly unco-ordinated, untrained, unfit, talentless supporters volunteer for amputation so that they could at least get out there and show some overpaid primadonna how to *try*. But Charlie didn't have to give his right arm to play for Arsenal. He had the skills, he had the swagger, he had the Arsenal tattooed on his heart, and he made that dreamlike, quantum leap off the terrace and on to the pitch. Wow.

Charlie was wonderfully unique. Although he wasn't the only elusive maverick floating through football in the early '70s, he was the only one who played for the team he had loved ever since he could remember loving anything. In the summer of 1953, with England in the throes of street parties to honour the Queen's coronation, Charlie the toddler went out to play dressed up as Jimmy Logie, the wizard who crafted Arsenal's attack of the day. Little did Mr and Mrs George realise that their boy would one day become the King of Highbury. A vintage shot from football's 1971 collection of gimmicky photographs depicts Charlie in full regalia: shimmering robe over his kit, jewelled crown atop his lank hair, orb in one hand and FA Cup in the other. His expression is something to behold, a cross between what the 'eck's this all about, I quite like being a King as it goes, and this is a right laugh.

With his supermodel style and mindboggling legs, he was every man on the North Bank's darling, worshipped by the very people he stood alongside as an impressionable nipper. One of the first games he saw, a 5–4 humdinger against Manchester City when David Herd scored a hat-trick for Arsenal and Denis Law notched three for the visitors, stands out in Charlie's memory. He was ten years old and he was entranced: 'Denis Law and Jimmy Greaves were my idols as footballers, because you always want to see goalscorers and flamboyance in people. Greaves was an immaculate goalscorer, he never had to strike the ball hard, everything looked easy. Law was a dynamite figure with the blond hair; he stuck out, and he'd always do something you would either like or dislike but you'd remember it. He was an electric player for me. And he was a bit naughty and that appealed to me too.' The superstar, the showman, the rascal; Charlie knew what he wanted to emulate.

Like all the best heroes, Charlie was a natural. Legends have so much more allure when their gifts come personally wrapped up by God. Learning they go through all the same mundane dross as the rest of us – work, problems, unpleasant bodily functions – is an appalling discovery. How shocking it was for all those Elvis fans to come to terms with the fact his final energy was expended on the toilet, his farewell royal evidence apparently left in the bowl. Perhaps that's why so many refuse to accept he is gone. It couldn't be *him*. The King wouldn't do *that*.

Anyway, Charlie's brilliance was inborn. He wasn't interested in the old adage about practice making perfect because he didn't need to be. 'Football was just easy for me,' he shrugs, emanating nonchalant simplicity. 'I wasn't the greatest player in the world and I wasn't the worst but I could play football. I just saw things. It just happened. I never had to work at anything, I never worked at striking a ball, any ability I had was absolutely natural.' Lucky Arsenal. This prodigy whose feet cast a spell on a football was on their doorstep, mesmerising his way round the playground of Holloway School. Both Don Howe and Bob Wilson coached there and they were instantly struck by Charlie's innate talent. The teachers who tried to guide him through the academic arts were less impressed by his efforts and Charlie was expelled. No matter. He didn't need to know about other stuff, he knew about football and anything else was insignificant. Anyway, he reckoned authority was bunk. Charlie was a rebel and his cause was Arsenal.

Nothing fazed him. For most fans, the experience of coming into close contact with players you revere from afar can reduce you to a state of quivering anxiety. Yeah, sure. Charlie simply climbed up onto the mental pedestal which separates the admirers from the admired. 'I wasn't really a shy person,' he says, master of understatement. 'I never felt out of place. I've always mixed with people a bit older than myself and as a kid I always played with older people so I never felt inferior. Once you step over the line you get a buzz, you know? In a funny way, it's a cockiness from knowing what I could do when I played football and I always had confidence in my own ability. There wasn't anything I didn't think I could do with a ball. That was my philosophy.' He breezed into the dressing-room oozing the cheek of the Artful Dodger and the arrogance of Top Cat. Not only did he enter into the banter immediately, he started plenty. 'He was just Charlie off the terraces when he was walking about in an Arsenal blazer,' remembers Frank McLintock, 'If he didn't like somebody he'd let them know, "*You're a tosspot*" and all that, and he never lost his brashness at all. He was a right outspoken sod, but that's what made him a special player.'

The impact he made on the Arsenal backchat scene was nothing compared to the shockwaves he caused at the training ground. Some of the experienced pros had never seen anything like him. His party piece was to launch the ball into orbit, eye it indifferently as it sped down, then kill it stone dead. A doddle. He had swank, he had subtlety of touch, he had substantial thighs, qualities which fused to give him the power to unleash those trademark missile shots. Charlie sprayed passes around with the ease of a Beckenbauer, knocked volleys over his shoulder and into the roof of the net like a Best, swerved past challenges like a Cruyff . . . McLintock and McNab glanced at each other in amazement . . . and then he swore like Johnny Rotten. Good old Charlie, all the skill in the world and none of the sophistication.

But Charlie had glamour. What is it with footballers and hair? Charlie's flowing unkempt mane had the desired effect. He stood out from the other players on the pitch, however inventive they might have been – and Peter Marinello was particularly imaginative. Charlie's style made a statement, however: *I don't care, I don't pose, I just let it all happen.* Without even trying, the rebel was perpetuating his own myth.

Strip away the layers of bravado and way down in the pit of Charlie's stomach was evidence of nerves: 'I used to be physically sick before games. Frank said to me years ago, "I know there's a lot of pressure on you because you're a local lad." I never actually felt it but I couldn't eat before a game because I used to burn a lot of acid up in my body. Once I was out there I was okay. I've never felt in awe of anybody, never ever in my life. There was nothing that any footballer could do that I felt I couldn't do. Whether that was right or wrong, it's a good attitude to have.' His unwavering belief endeared him to his team-mates. If he was having an average game compared to the grandiose heights he could achieve, Bob Wilson used to get hold of him at half-time, urging him, coaxing him, pushing him to find the magic. 'He had an amazing ability, even if he'd played badly, to remember the one great ball he'd hit,' smiles Wilson, 'so he'd say, "*Yeah, well what about that ball . . .*" and he would have hit a pass no one else could hit. That was great. Charlie had the strut at 19.' As if being a local hero wasn't reason enough, the lethal combination of impertinence and brilliance guaranteed cult status.

The Double side, although they were better footballers than they are credited for as is Arsenal's way, were defiance personified. They could crush teams (for instance, Arsenal 4 Manchester United 0; Arsenal 6 West Brom 2; Arsenal 4 Everton 0) and they could grind down teams (exemplified by a proliferation of single-goal triumphs). If there wasn't the freedom to be fancy, they would be functional, whatever it took to win the points. Charlie was Arsenal's wildest of wild cards. He, above all, had the knack for the unpredictable flash of genius necessary to unlock the stiffest of games. And he had one more priceless asset which made the North Bank swoon: he was a nutter. He didn't come from the school of luxury entertainers; he also saw the beauty of getting stuck in.

'There's an aggressive streak inside most people. I like the physical part of the game – I think that's missing today. At times it gives you a bit of a buzz if you get a bit excited when you're playing,' Charlie cracks into a wicked laugh. As a young player, and a southern softy and cocky cockney at that, he sometimes had to deal with hefty treatment from the era's hard men. Charlie could clearly take care of himself, but it was reassuring to know his guardian angel was never far behind. Arsenal looked out for each other on the pitch; John Radford ensured nobody took advantage of Ray Kennedy, and Peter Storey kept his eye on anyone who took liberties with Charlie. 'Peter wasn't a dirty player as such – he was a great defender who was great at getting tackles in – but he could see what was happening and if he saw someone was getting out of order he'd try and put a mark on them,' Charlie explains, 'We weren't a really dirty side but we were aggressive. If it's channelled in the right areas you get respect out of people. We had a great rapport: all for one and one for all.'

★

On the opening day of the Double season Bertie Mee showed faith in his young upstarts. Rice, Kelly and George were in the starting line-up at Goodison Park, all of them raring to prove they should stay there. Not before time, reckoned Charlie, who thought his name should have graced the team sheet for years. 'Bertie Mee's attitude was no rushing, you play and rest a bit, and I don't agree with that. If you're good enough, you play. I possibly could have been an even better player if I'd have played even younger when the club was struggling and I was confident.' And so to Everton, reigning champions. *Good luck, Pat! Go for it, Eddie! Break a leg, Charlie!* Arsenal's maestro is intent on imposing himself on his illustrious opponents. But Charlie's bold attitude to goalscoring, for once, costs him dearly. In pouncing for an equaliser, he was pounced upon by Everton's goalkeeper, Gordon West. 'I sort of went to get up and I couldn't,' he says glumly.

His sock and boot were a ragged mess. 'I thought, "Me shinpad must be down there," but I had a double fracture of my right ankle. There was pain there but you just get on with it, don't ya. I got carried off. It was a bit of a blow for me because pre-season that year I was really on top of my game, really felt good. All of a sudden you get a kick right up the arse, everything you've done just goes *bang*. But, saying that, the goal was important to score, you don't worry about what happens. Then Big Ray came in the side, formed a great partnership with Raddy, and scored plenty of goals.'

Charlie found himself in the strange position of being back in the stands supporting the lads. Having experienced football on the other side of the barrier, he had to reconcile team concerns and personal ambitions. 'It's very difficult because you always want them to win. But if someone has come in and taken your place – and he was doing ever so well, Ray – you think "How am I going to get back in the team?"' The answer was to put Charlie back in but not at Kennedy's expense, giving him instead a new role lurking behind the attack. Leaving one of the two burgeoning hotshots out would have been a shameful waste of Arsenal's resources, so Don Howe delved into his box of tactical tricks to accommodate them both. 'They talk today about these players dropping off – Zola, Cantona, Bergkamp – but we were doing that 25 years ago with Charlie George,' remarks the coach. 'And he was *superb*. Yes, he scored great goals, but he was the crucial link between the back and the front as well.'

As for Charlie, he couldn't care less where he played as long as he could feel the thrill of foot on ball in front of a purring crowd. 'I could play either up front or midfield. It didn't matter, I always felt football was easy; if you give me the ball I will do the work. I only want the ball, then I will do whatever you want me to do with it.' Okay, Charlie, what we want you to do is pick up the ball on the halfway line, run like a gazelle towards the opposition box, then shoot like a hunter. Fine. No problem. Charlie did exactly that to mark his return to action in the fourth round of the FA Cup against Portsmouth.

The Cup was the perfect platform for Arsenal's virtuoso. The roulette wheel of knockout competition stimulated his creativity and stoked his conviction. Under the spotlight of the big occasion are reputations created or killed. With each round, so Charlie's notoriety grew. Having got back into the scoring groove in the fourth round, he netted winners in the next two stages. And a couple of them were the kind of gems only Charlie could unearth.

Maine Road was not the most appetising draw for Arsenal, especially after a biblical flood which turned the pitch into an Olympic swimming-pool. 'I don't know whether Malcolm Allison had flooded it at the time, I think they had a couple of players injured,' wonders Charlie, 'but when it rains in Manchester . . . *it rains.*' The game, which had already been postponed once, was played under floodlights on a ghastly northern night. Frank McLintock felt it was time to play mind games with the joker in Arsenal's pack, just in case he wasn't feeling inspired. 'I hope you play well tonight, Charlie,' warned the captain, 'I was talking to Malcolm Allison and he doesn't rate you at all. He reckons you can only last about 30 minutes, he thinks you'll die a death, typical cockney.' Charlie turned the air in the dressing-room blue, then promptly went out and upstaged City's stars Franny Lee, Colin Bell and Mike Summerbee, with a stellar performance.

'I scored a free-kick and in the second half I broke from the halfway line and scored again,' elucidates Charlie, as if it was as simple as singing in the rain. 'We really played well. They scored a late goal but sometimes you just know you're not going to get beat. It was a funny set-up; if we scored first we never thought we'd lose.' McLintock, of course, hadn't spoken to City's manager before the game and he took great delight in telling Allison and George afterwards.

The semi-final pitted Arsenal against Stoke, the team whose 5–0 demolition job had rocked the lads in the league earlier in the season. Nightmare start: 2–0 down at half-time and on the way to another drubbing. What's more, both goals were gifts, one from Peter Storey and the other from Charlie with a wayward backpass. It was an afternoon ruled by nerves and Arsenal were losing theirs. The legendary Gordon Banks in the Stoke goal was also twitchy, and almost redressed the gaffes deficit with some hot-potato handling. So close to Wembley, the tension was getting to everyone. Back in the dressing-room crockery was smashed, tempers soared, and Arsenal, in particular old Ice Eyes Storey, emerged refocused. 'He was one of the most amazing characters,' reflects Bob Wilson. 'Off the field he was shy, but put him on a field and there was a transformation. He was like Robert De Niro, the good-looking, dark-haired charming guy – and all of a sudden he was an assassin. *You stand clear.* People classed him alongside the assassins of his day and he had more ability than he was given credit for. It was real passion with Peter. He just wanted to win.' Storey demonstrated all his deft talent with a fierce long-range drive to make it 2–1, then all his deadly nerve with an injury-time penalty. Hillsborough shook to the sound of thousands of knocking knees, every eye boring in on Storey, and the hitman hit home. All right, it wasn't the most clinical spot-kick in the world, but who cares? The Double dream remained alive.

The replay was a one-sided affair. No nerves this time. And Charlie soon got over his Hillsborough clanger: 'The first touch I got was a 60-yard backpass to the goalkeeper. I was very conscious of what had happened in the previous game and I did it just to prove to myself that everything was going to be all right. You get over something. You made a mistake but you've got to get on with it, you're not going to change the course of history because whatever's happened happened. We won the game 2–0, quite comfortably in the end. George Graham got a great header from about 18 yards then Ray got the second. We felt we were never going to lose. Again we went in front and didn't lose.'

So Mee's men were bound for the Twin Towers, and after Leeds and Swindon they were praying for third time lucky against Liverpool. Although Wembley is only a few miles from Highbury, it had been the most arduous of journeys, as the velvet hat conjured up away draws in every round. The boys took the scenic route via the delights of Yeovil, Portsmouth, Manchester, Leicester, Sheffield and Birmingham. They had every right to be exhausted before they even arrived at their final destination. And all along, the Cup had been a diversion, light relief from the rigours of the league chase. Arsenal used only 16 players during that epic 64-game season, and considering Marinello and Nelson made only three and four appearances respectively, the Double was won by a hard core of 14 players. Their efforts were little short of phenomenal.

★

In the midst of the madness in the visitors' dressing-room at White Hart Lane, God knows how anyone heard the telephone ring. 'Bill Shankly here, put that man Bertie Mee on the line,' commanded football's psychological mastermind. 'A tremendous performance, Bertie, magnificent. You may even give us a game on Saturday.' Mee, we can safely assume, was in the mood to take on anyone. And Charlie was in the mood to go home to his mum and dad's flat. Were you saving yourself for something, Charlie? 'I don't know what for,' he quips, with a teasing laugh.

Shankly wasn't the only one to indulge in mental trickery. 'We got him back at the final,' Bob Wilson recalls. 'As we'd been at Wembley twice before, we knew that because of the drill with the royal party they keep you waiting in the tunnel with the cameras on you for far too long. You can wet yourself there – some players really lose it. We refrained from going out. The FA official knocked on the door . . . "Sorry, we're not ready," said Bertie, "Just doing my team-talk." The second knock and Frank made out he had a problem with a stud. The Liverpool lads were out there for ages and Shanks knew exactly what we were up to. We saw him fuming when we came out.' The players emerged to a collage of red and white and yellow and blue vibrant in the scorching sunshine. Charlie, having vomited his jitters out in the dressing-room toilet, was as saucy as ever. His first match at Wembley, beamed to 400 million around the world. 'I wasn't nervous. I just wanted to go and get started so we could get the game over, win the Cup and go and have a drink,' he says.

Maybe it was appropriate that after Arsenal's mammoth season the game to seal the Double should go into extra-time. It ought to have been wrapped up in 90 minutes, but the Wembley hoodoo wasn't going to be exorcised that easily. A couple of George thunderbolts, Armstrong's free header, Kennedy in the clear, two close shaves from Graham . . . Not ready, said the net, must work harder. 'We were all very well aware of what we could do but then Liverpool wasn't a team that was going to lie down,' George tuts. Indeed they didn't. Steve Heighway twinkle-toes into the Arsenal area and rifles that shot most dreaded by goal-keepers, squeezed between body and near post. Bob Wilson, having had such a dazzling season, deserved better.

'*Oh no*,' George groans, reliving the memory. He sighs and lets his head droop. 'There was something there and all of a sudden it was taken away from you.' But Arsenal knew the routine. You take your knocks on the chin, then launch straight into the sucker punch. Play Brian Moore: 'Radford, back over his head. Kelly is right in there, playing much more as a striker in this extra-time . . . AND IT'S THERE! GEORGE GRAHAM! It's George Graham who got the touch and makes it 1–1!' In fact it was George Graham who sold the greatest dummy of all time, kidding everyone in the stadium that he'd got the final stroke. Or did he? He swears to this day his foot connected with the ball, even though television evidence later gave the goal to Kelly. 'It didn't matter, we'd scored,' grins Charlie. 'George probably claimed it because he realised he'd had a good game and he thought he might clinch the Man of the Match award.

'Pushing forward and trying to score in extra-time is very difficult. It was so hot, like a cauldron. The heat was so intense it was unbelievable. The day absolutely drains you. The 90-minute period I've played as well as anyone, but in extra-time I was tired. I swapped over and moved up front. I think Geordie dropped back. I was a little bit knackered but I could always find the strength to hit one from 20 to 30 yards. It was never a problem. It was easy for me to hit a ball, no matter how far or what distance.'

Play Brian Moore: 'Graham. Radford. Charlie George. Radford. Oh, Charlie George, who can hit 'em . . . OH, WHAT A GREAT GOAL, CHARLIE GEORGE! WELL, WHAT A FABULOUS GOAL BY GEORGE! CLEMENCE HAD NO CHANCE WITH THAT!'

It is stunning. And what follows is equally staggering: Charlie is floored by his own knock-out blow. It remains one of the game's enduring images, imprinted on the minds of football fans regardless of club. Like Maradona's Hand of God, or Cantona's martial artistry, like Schumacher's GBH on Battiston, or Gascoigne's tears, like Ronnie Radford's missile for Hereford or Roger Milla's bum wiggle. There, alongside them, is Charlie, a symbol of everything that is precocious about football and life, lying flat with his arms outstretched out on the Wembley turf. The best thing about it is the look on his face. It's as if he's saying, well, what did you all expect? It just happened, didn't it? The epitome of cool.

We've all done it. We've all scored a goal somewhere – in the playground, in the garden, in the front room, wherever – and fallen prostrate to the ground, being Charlie. I know I have.

Charlie is as casual about it as ever. 'I was fortunate the way it dropped to me. You get the accolades but it was a team performance and it wouldn't have mattered whoever scored as long as we won. I've always tried to play for the supporters because at the end of the day I've been a supporter myself. I always feel you're giving them something back. If you score and just run back to the halfway line it's absolute bollocks. There's no feeling. I always felt the rapport with the crowd. The word "superstar" is probably used very lightly; the few superstars about were the likes of Best and Law. I enjoyed it – if you don't, there's no point in playing.'

Charlie, aged 20, his first Wembley final, is a winner. Frank McLintock, aged 31, his fifth Wembley final, is a winner too. After over 60 games tackling and running and shouting, after extra-time in 90 degrees, he charges up those steps to get hold of the FA Cup like a man possessed. Then suddenly it hits him. 'I was a spent force, a goner. My candle [he snaps his fingers] burned out. I gave absolutely everything until I had nothing left to give.' That night, the man who had been out until dawn after Tottenham was a zombie. That night, Charlie didn't go home. He went mad.

In 1975 he was sold to Derby. Never has an ex-player had such a welcome at Highbury revisited in another team's colours. When he came out on to the pitch so did half the crowd, brandishing gifts for our Charlie. Before kick-off he stood there with his hands full of flowers, champagne, and even a bottle of light ale.

Critics say Charlie George never fulfilled his true potential. He could have ended up playing for Barcelona. He ended up playing for Dundee United. He shrugs. 'I could have been a better player, I suppose. People seem to have said that about me. I'm quite happy about my life, I don't complain about anything, just sort of get on with it.' So Charlie drifted about, from one shenanigan to the next. One of his fingers is missing, from the knuckle bone upwards, which he claims is the result of a lawnmower accident. It's debatable whether even the lawnmower believes him. He always was a rogue.

Now he's back where he started, a face going about his business in Islington, watching the Arsenal on Saturdays. Wherever he goes he's still patted on the back for that goal. If you had a pound for every time it's been mentioned to you, eh, Charlie? 'I'd be quite wealthy now. I think it's quite nice to be recognised. I come from the area and I talk to people from five-year-old kids to 70-year-old women and they always want to talk about football because I'm a local lad. It stands me in good stead that people recognise you scored the goal which enabled the club to win the Double. No matter where I go now – I watch Arsenal approximately 80 per cent of games home and away – I'm recognised and I enjoy it. I've been a supporter and then I played and now I'm a supporter again. You could ask international players who've played here and they'll tell you this is the best there is. It's the greatest game ever, especially if you're at one of the big clubs. Arsenal is without doubt one of the biggest clubs and always will be.

'I get a tremendous buzz being here all the time. I enjoy coming to the club and I get immense pleasure out of watching Arsenal. I only watch Arsenal, I don't really watch too much other football. I still get the same feeling when I see Arsenal play and score – the likes of Bergkamp who is, for me, a phenomenal player, and Wright, who is probably the greatest goalscorer the club has ever had. Even now when I watch the game if we lose I just want to go home, feeling terrible.' Fancy Charlie George just going home after a game.

He is the most Arsenal of Arsenal men. It could never be any other way. 'I don't know why I was dressed up as Jimmy Logie in 1953. Why an Arsenal player? Why not a Tottenham player or a West Ham player? Perhaps there was something someone knew was going to happen.'

Character

PAT RICE

Arsenal 3 Manchester United 2
12 May 1979

Jennings, Rice, Nelson, Talbot, O'Leary, Young, Brady, Sunderland,
Stapleton, Price (Walford), Rix

The niggly sparring match with Alex Ferguson in the closing stages of Arsène Wenger's first season was the latest weave in an intricate tapestry of intriguing clashes between Arsenal and Manchester United, London's aristocrats versus the Cocks of the North. It's a contest which is charged by history, and the roots were planted on the first day of February 1958, when Highbury hosted an unforgettable game. At the time, nobody realised it would mark the last appearance on English soil of the Busby Babes before half the team perished in the Munich aircrash. Everybody was simply entranced by a classic which United won by the odd goal in nine. None more so than an eight-year-old football-mad lad from Belfast over in London visiting his brothers, who bunked into Highbury to watch his heroes. Like many Irishmen he was a Manchester United fan. His name was Pat Rice.

Ninety minutes later he was converted. He'd seen the team for him – he was Arsenal. It seems illogical that the experience of watching them lose 5–4 should persuade him to swap allegiances, but on closer inspection it's no surprise that the character Arsenal showed that day struck a chord with Rice. He was a boy with a never-say-die spirit and he saw that trait embodied in the team

76

in red and white. Trailing 3–0 to United, Arsenal roared back to life to make it 3–3; then, after another two blows, again the Gunners fought back. They were a team who flatly refused to give in. Pat liked that.

He showed the same plucky tenacity in his quest to become a footballer. If his contemporary Charlie George was blessed with abundant skills and never had to work at it, Pat was blessed with bloody-minded determination and had to slog till he dropped to improve his basic skills. He scampered with such persistence on his first day as an apprentice that he lost six pounds in weight, and when he arrived at the greengrocer's shop where he helped out during the afternoons, he slunk into the back room, lay down and went to sleep.

He was eleven when his family moved to the mainland and Rice's new home was on Avenell Road. At least he was in the right environment for football, in the very shadows of the stadium of his new favourite team. It made a change from Belfast where his opportunities had been restricted to kickabouts against a wall with a goal marked out. Two nights a week he trained at Highbury, and Pat was always there an hour early to run on his own until the other kids arrived, imagining he was a professional preparing for a First Division game. As an associated schoolboy he received two bob for the privilege. Fancy earning money to play at Arsenal.

'That was easy,' smirked Pat in the summer of 1971, reflecting on his league and FA Cup-winners' medals. He was talking to Dai Rees, a Gunners fanatic and the resident professional at the South Herts golf club where Arsenal chomped their pre-match meals. Rees, having won the British Open, was no stranger to success, and the Jack the Lad right-back was soon taught some home truths about sporting endeavour. 'Son, that doesn't mean nothing,' chided Rees. 'To prove that you're really great you've got to win again this season, and next season, and then the season after that. Then you'll be really great.'

Where do you go after the Double? Ignoring the remote possibilities that either your team assumes bionic powers or every single one of your challengers becomes lily-livered, you will in all probability fail to repeat the feat. In a perverse twist, Arsenal were on a collision course against their Double opponents in the following two seasons, Leeds in the 1972 FA Cup Final and Liverpool in the 1973 Championship race. In both Pat and the boys finished runners-up. Thanks for the advice, Dai.

Bertie Mee felt he had no option but to rebuild. Don Howe had sailed off to paddle West Brom's canoe and his replacement Steve Burtenshaw didn't have enough edge to get a winning response from the lads. Something had to give. McLintock and Graham were the first to go, soon followed by Kennedy. Having finished in the top two of a major competition for six consecutive seasons, the painful dismantling of the Double team was under-way. After such consistency, Arsenal began to crumble. Pat was downcast: 'I personally believe the team was broken up too early. Bertie had heard from the great managers like Bill Shankly and Harry Catterick that once you've won a Championship the best thing to do is get some of the old players out and some fresh faces in, and I think he did that too soon. There were times when we were really, really struggling and it definitely wasn't nice. But it's the old saying: if you've never experienced the hardship, you can't judge the good times.' In 1976 Arsenal slumped to shocking depths, finishing an abominable seventeenth in the league – *seventeenth!* – just one place off relegation – *relegation!!* – and were unceremoniously dumped out of the FA Cup in the third round, stuffed 3–0 by Wolves. It was an uncomfortable epilogue to Mee's Arsenal career.

'People were choked and we were absolutely gutted because we didn't know who was going to come in,' recalls Pat. 'There was speculation Bobby Campbell was going to take over or the Yugoslav Miljan Miljanic. It was unsettling.' What shockwaves if Arsenal had done something as innovative as appointing a foreign coach. As it was, they plumped for Terry Neill, the jovial Irishman who played for the club for over a decade, following in the comfortable tradition of keeping it in the family. Still, some had their doubts, wondering what the hell he was doing mana-ging at White Hart Lane if he was such an Arsenal man. A job's a job, I suppose. And the players' immediate reaction? 'Let me put it this way,' Pat muses, 'it was far from the best. We found it very strange him coming from Tottenham. I thought to myself, "There is nothing you can do about it. He's been appointed by the board of directors and you've just got to get on with it and see how things turn out." In fairness, while he was manager, we got to four finals.'

The brave new world looked suspiciously like same old Arsenal in Neill's first game, against Bristol City at home, and a groansome 0–1 beating. The team immediately picked up, taking eight points from the next ten. A delighted Neill waltzed into the boardroom. 'Well, chairman, how about that?' he beamed. Denis Hill-Wood nodded, replying, 'Marvellous, Terry. Only 30 more points to avoid relegation.'

Neill tore into the task of revitalising Arsenal. He was a serial transfer-dealer and immediately started shuffling the squad with the impulse of a high-risk poker player. He buzzed from the acquisition of Malcolm Macdonald, a glamorous £333,333-worth of bulldozing striker; took an almighty gamble with capricious Alan Hudson; and played a curious hand by nipping back to White Hart Lane to pick up Willie Young, six foot two, eyes of blue, after you, and not a popular man with the Arsenal faithful after some emphatically aggressive derby antics in the past. Big Willie withstood a thorny first season in N5 and, to his credit, came out the other side with cult status. Neill also invited Pat Jennings to move across North London so that the first three names on Arsenal's team sheet replicated that of Northern Ireland: Jennings, Rice, Nelson. It was an inspired signing. One of the greatest goalkeepers in the world, Tottenham had thought his career was winding down, yet he was still performing wonders at Highbury seven years later.

Neill was equally eager to sell and, before long, all but one of the remaining pieces from the Double jigsaw were lost. It speaks volumes for Pat Rice's durability that he survived two energetic shake-ups during the '70s. While more artistic players fell by the wayside, he ploughed on with his brand of unfussy, utterly reliable football.

All the early evidence suggested Neill's managerial affair with Arsenal was going to be like a celebrity romance, always on the verge of a storm, always a stylish high or a gobsmacking low, and always in the headlines. How boring. At the end of his first season he made one of his most prudent decisions by reclaiming a respected coach. His first choice was Dave Sexton, who took the opportunity to manage Manchester United instead, so Neill turned to Don Howe, who would again resuscitate Arsenal's strategy and spirit. 'That was the best thing Terry ever did,' suggests Pat, 'I knew the players would respond to him.' They did. Howe revelled in the task: 'I was very lucky that both the managers I worked with at Arsenal let me have my freedom with the team, which was fantastic. I appreciated that.'

Howe's return couldn't have come at a more opportune moment. The potential was clearly there but the mood was too turbulent for the fruits to bloom. Arsenal had a vintage crop of youngsters who needed guiding (Brady, O'Leary, Stapleton, Rix, Price), a group of experienced players who needed stimulating (Rice, Nelson, Jennings, Sunderland, Young) and a couple of big-shots who needed harnessing (Supermac and Huddy). Capers came to a head when Macdonald and Hudson were sent home from a pre-season tour of the Far East after one or two boozy misdemeanours too many. It would take more than that to ruffle Don Howe: 'When I came, I sat down with the players and said, "This is my second stint here. I believe in teamwork and spirit in a club and if we don't get those right we're never going to get any success. That's what we're aiming for, let's get on with it." As for the so-called difficult ones, no problem at all,' he says. 'In fact, they wanted to win as badly as anyone. All the little rumours you hear in football, within a few weeks I was thinking, "What was all that about?" I had one or two halfway-house chats with Malcolm and Alan, but they were fine.'

Nor could Pat find fault with Hudson's efforts. 'One of the best in training I was ever involved with,' he reckons. 'He might have had a good Sunday night – you could see it in his face – but he would come into training Monday morning and if you were doing any physical work he was at the front, leading the way.' Pat was, however, less convinced by Macdonald. 'I would have to say this, he was a great goalscorer.' He grins mischievously. 'That's it.'

It was a challenging time for Rice to be given the captaincy, and since his stubborn streak had led to the odd confrontation with Neill in the past, he was flabbergasted to be asked. 'Being an older player, if I didn't agree with something that the manager wanted done, I would tell him so. Never in a million years did I expect to be captain. All of a sudden it was upon me and I told all the players I wouldn't tell them any lies, and they knew that. Whatever was told to me was told to them. They knew I would stick up for them. At the same time, the management also knew that if I thought it was right I would say to the players: "Come on, this has got to be good for us." It wasn't all rebelling, rebelling, rebelling. If I thought something was brewing among the players, I would warn the management to watch out.'

Pat echoed Don Howe's sentiments about creating a strong togetherness, and he had been fortunate to learn all about that from Frank McLintock. Another stroke of luck was that the seven Irishmen in the team set the tone for chirpy banter. Whenever the team were on the coach, the Dubliners, folk crooners from the Emerald Isle, were favourites for the tape-machine. The English lads moaned, the Irish lads called for a vote, the hands went up and 'The Wild Rover' was on full blast. And if the team won, they would all be singing along on the way home, regardless of nationality. 'The comradeship was really good,' crows Pat.

Typical of Arsenal, the bond was tightened by an inglorious defeat. For Swindon 1969 read Ipswich 1978, and again a mood of heightened determination was forged in a subdued Wembley dressing-room. 'There were loads of people crying and I just went round with the champagne. "*Get it down you*," I said. "*Remember. Remember how you feel now. When the Cup run starts next season you can think back to this*." If the Ipswich game had been a league game and not an FA Cup Final, five players out there would not have played. Liam, Malcolm, Willie, Sammy and I played with injuries and had to have painkilling injections prior to the game.' Pat shakes his head and his voice becomes doleful, as if he's telling a sob story. 'Liam gave his medal away. He said he didn't do himself justice. He said "I'll be back next year."'

Brady, believing he had failed his team-mates, his club, his family and himself, vowed never again to chance his fitness in an important game. The following season, Arsenal's linchpin found himself 90 minutes away from an FA Cup Final return and feeling the effects of an ankle knock. Neill asked Brady if he was fit to play and the recently crowned Footballer of the Year put hand on heart to answer no. It was a brave decision, vindicated when his team-mates brushed Wolves aside 2–0 to set up Wembley revisited. Liam would have his day.

The final, against Manchester United, was the climax to what had been a riveting saga. If you win all your FA Cup-ties at the first time of asking, five games will see you through to the final; yet in 1979 it took Arsenal the same number of matches just to get past Third Division Sheffield Wednesday in the third round. After a compelling nine hours and 16 goals, the Gunners finally battered the sheer resistance of Jack Charlton's team into submission. Another highlight came at Nottingham Forest, when Arsenal became the first side to beat Brian Clough's men at the City Ground for almost two years. People muttered about Arsenal's name being on the Cup which, along with 'we'll be back next year', is one of the FA Cup's most over-optimistic platitudes. It's like saying there'll be another one along in a minute when you've just missed the 210. Then again, they talk about the luck of the Irish and, with the combined vibes of Pat, Pat, Sammy, John, David, Liam, Frank and Terry, Arsenal could will another bus round the corner. Perhaps their name was on the Cup after all.

But there was the waft of an ill wind swirling around Arsenal's Wembley build-up for one of the Irish contingent. Having scored a goal in a league match against Coventry, Sammy Nelson mooned at the North Bank. In spite of the hilarity it caused on the terrace, the old farts at the FA were not amused. Pat and the boys thought their reaction was ridiculous: 'It was a laugh and completely misunderstood. He's hit this shot and it flew in the top corner and his shorts have just gone down and up [Pat whips an imaginary pair of shorts off and on in a nano-second] and someone just managed to get the photograph. It was a joke – he was always joking.' There was concern that the FA punishment might ban Nelson from the Cup Final, but they restricted his suspension to two matches which left him a free man in time for

Wembley. And as for the small matter of a £750 fine . . . 'We tried to have a whipround for him and he wouldn't accept it,' smiles Pat, 'which I was pleased about.'

The Arsenal bus draws up at Wembley rocking to the familiar sound of The Dubliners. In contrast to the previous year, everyone is upbeat; now familiar with Cup Final glitz, the players could focus on rising to the occasion rather than being rattled by it. The biggest boost is that everyone is fully fit (except for Don Howe who feels poorly, but thankfully his brain rather than his brawn is all that's required). There are two changes to the 1978 team, Brian Talbot – who had arrived from last year's conquerors Ipswich – and Graham Rix for Macdonald and Hudson. Both are protagonists in the ensuing drama.

The captain is confident: 'We thought we had the capability of beating them. Definitely. Alan, Frank, Liam, Graham, and David Price were all playing well. All we had to do as a back four was stand firm and make sure we didn't concede any goals and it would only be a matter of time before one of those five stuck the ball in the back of the net.' Perfect. By half-time it's 2–0 thanks to a joint effort from Talbot and Sunderland (the former claimed it, the latter would later have his say) and a textbook header from Stapleton. Significantly, both goals were conjured by Arsenal's merlin, Brady. 'People got it all wrong with Liam. They thought the more they let him have the ball in the middle of the park, the safer they were in numbers behind,' Pat explains, 'but the lower half of his body was so strong he just ghosted past people and he had such a quick brain he could either play people in, play one-twos, float a ball in or score tremendous goals himself. United tried to put Lou Macari on him but they couldn't handle him at all.' Arsenal are imperious, the fans delirious. There is only one team that looks like scoring. 'Truthfully, I can't remember them putting us under pressure,' adds Pat. Five minutes to go and the fat lady is limbering up those vocal chords. 'Ee ay addio, we've won the Cup,' gloat the Arsenal masses, making sure she knows what to sing.

The reason an audience of millions is seduced by sport is

because it is the world's natural theatre. Unscripted, unpredictable, and, when it's at its most potent, so unbelievable you wonder if your eyes are deceiving you. Sport can grab control of your soul and drag it through a prism of emotion. And so it came to pass that Arsenal were yanked from a state of contented bliss to crushed desolation in the space of a minute. McQueen's goal is an irritation, a consolation for United, 2–1. But McIlroy's goal is devastation. 2–2. Shellshock.

'If the game had gone into extra-time I honestly believe they would have beaten us,' admits Pat. 'We were on a real downer, 2–0 up, coasting it, thinking we've only got another ten minutes left and we've won the Cup . . . and all of a sudden, *bang, bang*. I think we were really choked simply because of the amount of people McIlroy had beaten.' Pat flashes an incredulous look. 'That was never known, he's beaten Stevie Walford, Dave O'Leary, he's come inside and slipped it under Pat Jennings. It was people not marking, people being relaxed. I thought, *That's it. We've blown this*. But of course with Brady and Rixy out there it's never over.'

Within seconds of the restart the ball is at the master crafts-man's feet. One minute left on the clock. Yellow socks rolled down to his ankles, number 7 shirt flapping outside his shorts, he summons enough guts and guile to spirit the ball towards the danger zone. 'I just wanted to get the ball in their half because I thought they were likely to score again,' says Brady. He slips the ball to Rix, bursting along the left flank, who crosses for Sunder-land, bombing through the middle. The man with a bubble perm so extreme it pulsated like a jellyfish after an electric shock stretches every muscle, every tendon, every raw nerve in his right leg to smack the ball past Bailey. 3–2. Incon-bloody-ceivable.

Everyone's emotions are all over the place, including the Arsenal captain's. 'I know people who say they died and went to heaven in the space of two minutes. We felt that too. A friend of mine told me he didn't see the goal because he was crying. Head in his hands. I remember the ball going into Pat Jennings' hands and he threw it to me and I was trying to waste time. *Kick it in the corner, knock it back to Pat, do anything, just kill time*. The final whistle was simply relief and exhaustion. Christ. All the hard work is over now.' The first 85 minutes seemed so long ago it was hard to recall they had even existed. History would log this game as the five-minute final.

Rice virtually sprints up Wembley's 39 steps – 'I couldn't wait to get up there and get my hands on the Cup' – his adrenaline pumping so fast he doesn't dare pause to collect his medal. All he wants is to hoist the trophy in the air. 'I've got a picture of me holding the Cup and Prince Charles is trying to give me my medal.' He could wait. Protocol could take a running jump out the Royal Box. The lad who grew up in Avenell Road, whose first Arsenal experience was a meaningful match against Manchester United, had captained his club to triumph at their expense. Pat clutches the booty as if it is an extension of his body; he isn't best keen on giving it up for his team-mates to have a hold. 'Too right,' he barks. 'It was a fairy story, and it came true for me. I'm extremely proud.'

Having forced his colleagues to drink champagne a year before, this time they needed no invitation. 'I was a little bit inebriated in the dressing-room, I know that. Brian Talbot collapsed from exhaustion and at one stage they were thinking of taking him to the hospital because he had run so hard and covered so much ground. If he had gone we were all going with him because we had been through it all together.' Talbot made history by being the first man to aid the team he helped vanquish the previous year to become victors. Brady had a medal he could keep. O'Leary was a winner for the first time in what would be a distinguished 20-year Arsenal playing career. Rice, who had seen it all before with the Double, who said it was easy back in 1971, who subsequently lost another two FA Cup Finals, knew that it was bloody hard work. And well worth it.

★

Pat Rice has seen every Arsenal success since the 1970 revival (that's ten trophies) from the inside. In 29 years of service he has performed just about every role: youth-team player, reserve, first-team pro, captain, youth-team coach, assistant manager and even caretaker manager. He is now 48 and since the age of 15 he has only been away for four years. That was an eye-opener. 'When I

got to Watford they gave me my own training kit and I said:
"What's this for?" They said, "You wear one one day and the
other the next day. When you've worn it you take it home and
your missus washes it for you." I'd never had to bring a training
kit home to be cleaned. Here everything is done for you here.
Everything.'

He enjoyed his spell at Vicarage Road but when a Highbury
homecoming beckoned he was ecstatic. Don Howe installed him
as youth-team coach, and as one of only two prospects from the
1966 FA Youth Cup-winning side to make the grade (Nelson was
the other) he had first-hand knowledge of the Arsenal production
line. An important part of his job, he felt, was to teach his pupils
the extraordinary single-mindedness necessary to succeed. 'You
can see a player at 14 and think he's got a bloody good chance
and then all of a sudden he gets to 16 and you think, "What
went wrong with him?" Instead of being in bed going to sleep at
nine they could be in bed at it with their bird every night, for all
I know. It could be girlfriends or snooker – obviously they all
have to have outside interests, but moderation is the key. Sometimes to get the good things you've got to make sacrifices. It's
hunger, it's sensing a major opportunity.'

Pat's most recent graduate also completed the transition from
Youth Cup-winner to first team. Arsenal v Millwall, FA Youth
Cup Final 1994. Seventeen-year-old Stephen Hughes cracks the
ball into the back of the net to make it 3–0 to the Arsenal. The
lads are leaping about on the pitch and there, in the dug-out,
beams Pat Rice.

Under George Graham he was offered the reserve post but Pat
preferred the challenge of grooming the kids. And, echoing the
big boss man's style, he stood for no nonsense. 'You teach them
what you would consider to be the right way of being brought up
as an Arsenal youth-team player. Step out of line and you hammer
them. If I saw a youth player being out of order, I'd say, "Don't
do that." If he replied, "Ian Wright does it," I'd say, "Well, when
you play in the first team, you can do it. I'm telling you now,
don't do it." Hard but fair. With the first team you take a different point of view. I can't go to someone like Dennis Bergkamp
and say, "Don't do that." He can tell me to get stuffed.'

At Anfield, on 26 May 1989, Pat was on the bench next to George watching a team boasting his best boys, Adams, Thomas, Rocastle and Merson, pull off the result of all time. Arsenal and last-minute winners go together like ten pints and a curry – explosive and at the same time absolutely perfect. Pat had witnessed it ten years before thanks to Alan Sunderland, and he'd see it again thanks to Andy Linighan in 1993. (For the record, Storey in the 1971 FA Cup semi-final, Kennedy in the 1971 league finale, and Rocastle in the 1987 Littlewoods Cup semi all wrote unforgettable entries into the modern Arsenal late show hall of fame.)

Is this propensity for last-gasp goals merely a coincidence? Is there some esoteric masonic secret passed through the Marble Halls which gives Arsenal players the *je ne sais quoi* to invoke these stupefying strikes? Is there something in the water in N5? Pat believes this Herculean temperament is inbred, drummed in from the first moment a red-and-white shirt is worn. Nine out of the 17-strong squad used in 1989 were home-grown. Seven out of the 1979 FA Cup XI were home-grown. Eleven of the 16-man Double squad were home-grown.

'Even in this squad now, many of those that aren't home-grown, like Lee Dixon, Nigel Winterburn and Steve Bould, have been here ten years,' considers Pat. 'When they came they got that spirit of Arsenal within them. That's why, when you're bringing in players, you want them to have the spirit of your Tony Adamses. You're either a winner or you're not, and thankfully in recent years there have been quite a lot of winners in this club. The demands come not only from the supporters but from the players themselves.

'Everyone's up against it. No one likes you. *No one likes you.* The press don't like you, other fans don't like you . . . When we did the Double, we were Boring Arsenal and we had the second-highest goals-scored record. The last time we won the Championship in 1991 we had points deducted for the brawl, we had Tony gone inside, but we still went and won it and didn't get any credit. It's always the same. It builds us as players. It makes us stronger.'

When Arsène Wenger arrived, *un étranger* to the Arsenal

scene, Pat was on hand to introduce him to the club mentality. 'He knew all about the spirit,' affirms Rice, who doesn't feel a special responsibility to teach new recruits the Arsenal way because, in his opinion, if they couldn't perceive it, they wouldn't be here. 'They know. They play in the team and they see the spirit of the side, that they won't lie down and die, that even if they are two goals down they will have a go until the final whistle is blown. They know that if they don't respond the same way they ain't gonna be in the team. Look at Patrick Vieira. Mr Wenger knows what sort of players he is buying. He knew all about Patrick. He told me: "Patrick is a winner." In previous clubs Vieira might not have had the same feeling for the rest of the players but he knows now that he's in a side where if he's up against it, they are all behind him. It ain't just him battling on his own. He shows it and he's a star here now.' In Marc Overmars, Emmanuel Petit, Nicolas Anelka and co, Wenger continues to handpick players schooled in winning ways.

The combination of Arsène's modernistic approach and Pat's traditional virtues bodes well for Arsenal. Wenger was grateful to have Rice's assistance in his introductory season. 'My desire is to build a successful team but I also want to stay faithful to the spirit of the club,' expresses the French revolutionary. 'All my friends and family say there is something special in the stadium – nobody can explain it.' He smiles warmly as he surveys Highbury from the directors' box. 'Pat is a very big help to me because he is deeply, deeply Arsenal. He's so committed. He's a strong link between the past and the future.'

While Monsieur Wenger guides the club into a new era, Pat is alongside him to maintain the values of old. Who better to do that than a man who grew up on the club's camaraderie? Today, he can be found marching through the corridors joshing with all the staff he has known for years. 'Those people, even Maureen the tea lady, need to feel they are wanted. And she *is* wanted. It's not them and us, which is important because that's when you get a split in the camp and you can't have that anywhere inside the club. They all knew me as a player and as youth-team coach and they called me Pat or Ricey. Now I'm assistant manager that doesn't change. I don't want them to start calling me Mr Rice or boss or any of that crap. I can't really envisage a time when Arsenal aren't a part of my life. Even my family love the club – my wife and kids are potty about it. When I went to Watford, and obviously they were my number-one priority, the second question was *How did the Arsenal do?* If for some reason they severed my appointment here it still would be *How did the Arsenal do?* no matter where I was or what I was doing.'

The sound of a continental greeting spun with a rich Irish brogue reverberates round the Marble Halls. *'Salut!'* It sounds like Bob Geldof meets Inspector Clouseau, but it's Pat Rice. With a few Gallic shrugs he shares in a blast of banter with the kit-man and the travel club manager, and the subject is impending French lessons. Soon they'll be playing Edith Piaf on the team bus. No more Dubliners, then. Ricey's seen it all.

Look at That, Look at That

LIAM BRADY

Juventus 0 Arsenal 1
23 April 1980

Jennings, Rice, Devine, Talbot (Hollins), O'Leary, Young, Brady, Sunderland, Stapleton, Price (Vaessen), Rix

Steve Perryman hesitates, looks up for a fatal second to size up his options. Speed of thought, anticipation, instinct. It's what the brain perceives in those fractions of a moment which separates a good player from a sporting genius. Brady is light years ahead of him. He whips the ball from the Tottenham man's foot, takes two gentle touches to perfectly align the balance between body and ball, and then composes something beyond the imagination of everyone else in the stadium. He shoots with the outside of his left foot, leg following through almost 360 degrees to manipulate maximum topspin, and the ball curls like a crescent into the top corner.

Fumbling for the words to adequately describe visions of beauty is all too often an impossible task. John Motson commentating on *Match of the Day* didn't even try. He simply urged us to look at it, look at it. My advice to anyone who hasn't seen the goal is to get hold of the *History of Arsenal* video immediately and feast your eyes.

The game, incidentally, was an infamous 5–0 exhibition at White Hart Lane the day before Christmas Eve in 1978. With the kind of fanciful cockiness that follows such dreamy results, Arsenal supporters tucked into the turkeys harping that it could have been ten. Honestly, no exaggeration. Sunderland and Stapleton hit the bar, Price had a goal disallowed, and the keeper twice managed to fling himself in front of net-bound efforts. 'Spurs are absolutely overwhelmed,' gasped Motty. In the midst of this Arsenal barrage Liam eclipsed everything going on around him. Immune to the frazzled atmosphere, he ran the North London derby show, playing with the carefree charm of a child let loose in the park. Hat-trick hero Sunderland took the headlines but, unlike yesterday's news, Liam's poem in motion lives on in the memory.

What a fitting goal for a player whose nickname was Chippy. Sorry to shatter the romantic illusions but the moniker was earned by a ravenous appetite for fried potatoes. Apocryphal? Maybe.

From time to time, a player comes along for Arsenal who is *different*. So much so that even the club's worst detractors cannot help but like him. Those who compare the Highbury experience to sitting in front of a recently Duluxed wall are suddenly confronted with a Van Gogh. Like Alex James before him, Liam seduced the entire football public with his art, not just the goggle-eyed Arsenal faithful. In the history of the club, these two are the only players whose legendary status stretches beyond London N5, and indeed transcends English football and enters into the realms of the world game's greats. Pele, Platini, Puskas . . . Matthews, Muller, Maradona . . . Beckenbauer, Best – the name of Brady can sit alongside them without too much of an inferiority complex.

We never took much wooing with Liam. Before he'd even made his début we knew we were on to something, thanks to snippets in the programme which hinted at the meteoric progress of an Irish prodigy shooting through the ranks. '6 October 1973,' he reminisces, 'never forget it.' That was the date when a waif-like Liam introduced himself to the Highbury hordes against Birmingham City. As substitute, he had barely settled on the bench when Jeff Blockley twisted his knee after five minutes, up went the number 5 substitute's board, off limped one of the club's alarmingly awful buys, and on trotted the boy with the lyrical left foot who had been fostered by the Arsenal family. Observers were instantly entranced – Sammy Nelson watching from the stands reckoned he changed the course of the game – he had talent, he had temperament, he had long hair. The new Charlie George? Some even mooted the possibility of the new George Best because of the Irish connection. Before long it would be abundantly clear there was only one Liam Brady. He didn't have to imitate another because he had an aura all of his own.

After the match the press converged on him. Well, there was precious little else to set the pulse racing at Highbury that season. It was a knotty time for a 17-year-old to commence his career, Liam was on the cusp of greatness while the team was on the verge of falling apart. The period from signing for the club at the age of 13 to his breakthrough was marked by the rise and slump of success. 'I'd been coming to Arsenal since 1969 when they were a team that hadn't done too much. People said to me, "You're going to Arsenal? They never win anything," but then all of a sudden things started to happen, the Fairs Cup in 1970 and a year later the Double. It was a big club to be joining,' muses Liam. 'But when I came in, Arsenal's team was maybe a hangover from the great years which had gone on before. There was a transition going on but we didn't really understand that – we were only kids. I wanted to get out there and show people what I could do. If you're going to have a career in football you've got to be able to handle so-called pressures, things like playing in front of a big crowd for the first time, playing with people who had been heroes of mine like Charlie George, John Radford, Alan Ball and people like that. It wasn't a very harmonious period in the first team, people wanting to leave, but at that time all I could think was what an opportunity – let's make the most of it.'

Liam rose to prominence during the era when the Dutch were wowing the world with total football. This was a shock. We thought defenders were supposed to be firm and committed and we forgave them their occasional clumsiness; strikers were there for the glory and we didn't object if they ducked out of tackling; as for midfield, you had your generals, your hardmen, your creators . . . Liam was our total footballer. His passing repertoire was virtuosic, his dribbling was mesmeric, he could win the ball, shield the ball, distribute the ball with complete control. There was something ethereal about the way he played, although anyone who thought his slender build meant he lacked strength was missing the point. 'You see these scraggy kids arrive from school and 12 months later the top half is still skinny but the legs have become honed and muscular,' explains Bob Wilson. 'When Liam arrived he was like a pencil, but look at his thighs during his playing career – tremendous power.' Artists sometimes fall by the wayside because they don't have the resistance to cope with the artisans. It took a heck of an opponent to knock Brady off the ball.

Anyway, the beefiest lads are not always the most courageous, and there was nobody more appropriate for Liam to learn from on that front than the feisty Alan Ball. By Christmas time 1975 the QPR of Bowles, Francis and co were outmanoeuvred by a midfield duo hailed in the media as 'The sorcerer and his apprentice'. Ball was eager to help the lad, impressed by the fact his gifted protégé hadn't been 'brainwashed' by coaching and had his own mind. (Liam always had a wilful streak. He was but a bairn when he was expelled from school because of his football. Chosen to captain Ireland youths on the same day as a college match, his teacher ordered him to turn his back on his country or face the consequences. The Green shirt called. Liam found another school.)

Experience taught him how to reconcile two of his contradictory sides, the sensitivity and the steel, and both were used in tandem to wonderful effect. 'There was never any doubt he would be a great because not only did he want to be a fine player, *he wanted to win*,' Don Howe declares. 'There was no messing about with the players around him – he used to tear strips off them to get it right.' For Liam it was perfectly natural to muscle into heated team discussions, be it with his juniors like John Devine and Steve Gatting, his elders like Hudson and Macdonald, or even the boss Neill. By the time he had reached the sage old age of 22 he was one of the senior pros in the squad. An aesthete with attitude. Is it any wonder he had us all spellbound?

★

The mental dilemma we must unravel with all our heroes is that they are transitory. We give them unconditional love until they disappear from our lives (we never walk out on them, incidentally). Suddenly we are left carrying all this excess affection and struggling to find an outlet. Throwing it at somebody else on the rebound is a wholly unsatisfactory solution. *Here, John Hollins, Brian McDermott, have seven years of absolute adoration. Go on, take it, it's yours now.* It doesn't work like that.

It was the season when Brady was at the pinnacle of his powers for Arsenal, crystallised by his ravishing goal at White Hart Lane (and raving celebration where he ran the length of The Shelf blowing kisses to the Tottenham fans, *touché*), and climaxed by his captivating Wembley wizardry against Manchester United. And then he told us he was leaving us. At the precise moment we were all so hopelessly besotted with him.

The trouble was that Arsenal was Liam's girl next door, his first love. They had been together a long time, grown up together, and now he wanted to broaden his horizons. During the summer of '79, still basking in the FA Cup glow, the hacks picked up on the fact Liam had one year left on his contract. 'Instead of being cagey and cute and saying, "I'll wait and see what comes," like I do nowadays, I said, "Well, I really fancy playing abroad." The following season wasn't really a settled time for me,' Liam reflects. 'I don't know whether I was naïve or just honest, but I admitted to the Arsenal fans I was going to be leaving at the end of that season. I could sense their attitude changed a wee bit towards me. Deep down, they knew I loved them and I knew they loved me, but it's only natural, isn't it? *Why do you want to leave us?* It played on my mind, but they didn't know what was going on behind the scenes. From then on it was will-he-won't-he and I didn't play that well until maybe the second half of that season.' The year was punctuated with whispers and counter-whispers about a new contract, a labyrinth of rumours about where, when and if he would go.

Liam's restlessness was as ill-timed as a Salvador Dalí clock. When his Arsenal affair was in its infancy the team were cracking

up, and now he was contemplating splitting just as the lads began
to gel. 1979–80 was fast turning into a sensational season as the
Gunners launched an all-out attack on the silverware, reaching
the European Cup-Winners' Cup Final, FA Cup Final, League
Cup quarter-final and pushing Liverpool hard in the league.
Brady devotees were buoyed by fresh hope – perhaps a medal or
two would sway him to stay, and it would be too surreal for
Arsenal to end up empty-handed.

During that colossal campaign the lads produced one performance to rank with the might of Anderlecht and the marvels of
the Double, a victory which carried turn-of-the-decade Arsenal
onto an untouched plateau. A Cup-Winners' Cup semi-final
against . . . Juventus. At long last, cheered the lads, a name
worthy of the so-called *glamour* of European football which had
so far seemed like a mythical ruse. After three hostile trips into
the Eastern Bloc the previous year, the first stop of the European
tour was Fenerbahce, during a period of political unrest and cur-
fews in Turkey – jokes about *Midnight Express* went down only
moderately well. The next round took Arsenal back through the
Iron Curtain to gloomy Magdeburg, a grim prospect on the back
of a fragile 2–1 advantage from the first leg. Goals from Brady
and Price in an intense 2–2 draw were enough. Gothenburg was
the next port of call, no fears on the football front after a 5–1
steamroller at Highbury, but terrifying moments on the flying
front when, approaching ice-bound Sweden, the pilot of the air-
craft advised everyone to take precautions for an emergency landing. Several thousand despairing prayers later the plane was safely
grounded. Thankfully, it had been a false alarm.

Surviving all those scrapes had hardened Arsenal's fortitude,
and they needed every ounce of resolve for the semi-final. Neill's
daring team were pitted against the power of Giovanni Trappa-
toni's Juventus. A collection of internationals, a theatrical stadium,
a noble history, and a daunting European record. Arsenal's young
buccaneers against Italian sophisticates, it had the making of a
battle and a half, and so it proved.

A tense first-leg confrontation at Highbury set the tone, the
visitors demonstrating they had the strategy and savagery to
knock Arsenal out. Their masterplan was working a treat. Lead-

ing 1–0 from a penalty, although Arsenal peppered their goal, the bolt, as they say in Italy, was locked. Red frustration snapped into fury when Roberto Bettega assaulted the nimble spidery legs of David O'Leary. Neill went barmy. 'We have taken the studs out of O'Leary's legs and given them back to Bettega,' he stormed afterwards, 'That was one of the most vicious fouls I have seen in 20 years in the game.' At least a modicum of justice was restored when the villainous striker nodded the ball into his own net in the final minutes for 1–1. Still, by then the damage had been done, not merely to Arsenal's centre-half but to Juventus's pride. They bristled for days about Neill's attack on their beloved Bettega. A vast banner proclaiming 'Neill the dog', together with violent catcalls, awaited him in Turin. He'd get his come-uppance, of that they were convinced.

The English change into shorts at the first sign of sunshine, the Irish brew the best Guinness in the whole wide world, the Scots watch their purse-strings, and the Italians don't lose at home in European football. Cultural stereotyping, crassly facile though it is, exists for a reason. It's largely true. So Arsenal jaunted off to Turin in the knowledge that Juventus had only ever lost once in Europe at the Stadio Communale, never to an English team, and never in the last decade. So how do you prepare to do the illogical? 'We had a lovely time, we stayed at a super training camp in Asti for three days and enjoyed ourselves. We ate stacks of pasta, drank stacks of red wine and it really topped us up,' smiles Don Howe. 'It was just the right thing to do.'

23 April. Juventus away. Seventy thousand feverish Italians soon shake the lads out of their relaxed calm. The *bianconeri* trumpet their place in the final before the kick-off as Arsenal enter the arena to the imposing sight of a myriad Roman candles, the brutal rhythm of firecrackers ringing in their ears. Liam turns round to Rixy and grins, 'I fancy playing here.' Welcome to the big time.

Before long, says Liam, the smoking clamour eases into deafening quiet. 'We dominated Juventus and the crowd were silenced for 90 minutes. They had nothing to get worked up

Arsenal are back. Frank McLintock, and the Fairs Cup, are carried on the shoulders of the crowd

Bertie Mee cuddles Frank after winning
the league in 1971

Frank on the ball

Geordie, Geordie Armstrong on the wing

Charlie George, who can hit 'em, hits the deck, then shares some of that Double magic with the captain

Born is the King of Highbury

Pat Rice, an Arsenal kind of guy

Rice, Stapleton, Rix, Talbot, Jennings and O'Leary soaking up the 1979 FA Cup

Brady, a gem in a 5–0 drubbing at White Hart Lane

The maestro's final number. Liam waves farewell

about because their team sat back. We noticed at Highbury that they certainly weren't an absolutely devastating side and we'd nothing to fear. Don Howe did a marvellous job over there, psyching us up to go and win it, and they played into our hands, typical Italians. I came to know the coach the following year and he probably set it out that, having got the away goal, they don't concede a goal at home. They were aiming for 0–0, no doubt about it.' Rather than risk leaving any defensive gaps they play with safety in numbers, so Arsenal have to attain a level of cunning they never knew they had to unlock the infamously jammed bolt.

Howe is a man with a plan. 'We had our wingers and full-backs rotating and they didn't know what to do. They were so man-for-man-orientated that when the player they were marking went somewhere else, they had no idea. They kept looking across to the bench and, with the greatest respect to Trappatoni, he didn't know what to do.' This is all rather an inconvenience to the Italians, but 0–0 is 0–0 after all and the deadlock remains intact.

Arsenal press incessantly, creating a series of chances, with Liam supreme in midfield. He dazzles: 'I went close a few times from distance, hitting a few good shots from outside the area, and Frank went close three times, but Zoff was magnificent in goal. It just seemed we were never going to get there, until five minutes from the end, a magical move from Rix and Stapleton down the left, a great ball in from Rixy – not unlike the move to win the Cup Final – and there was Paul Vaessen, who was big enough to be able to go *thump* and head it in. They just lay on the ground, Juventus, so we knew we'd done it.'

Vaessen, the 18-year-old substitute who had blown up the invincible Italian machine, is swamped by blissed-out team-mates. All except Liam, who runs to his Arsenal soul-mate Rix, acknowledging the glory of football's creation, without which you have no execution. They embrace, sharing the moment as if there is nobody else in the stadium. The 70,000, who had been baying for the final whistle a minute before (the noisiest they were all game) are reduced to frozen disbelief.

'For me that was probably the biggest match we ever won for

Arsenal,' Liam claims. 'If I had to name my most outstanding game, I would name that one in Turin. It wasn't on television, there were very few Arsenal supporters there, Nottingham Forest won in the European Cup the same night to go into the final so they got all the attention, whereas our feat was bigger than anybody's. It was as momentous as anything I'd been involved in either in international or domestic football, including the Cup against Man United. It was a mountain to overcome, and Arsenal have this habit of doing just that.'

In his book *Steaming In*, Colin Ward, one of the 200-odd Londoners in Turin, recalls making a break from the post-match mean streets by jumping into a taxi. *Arsenal numero uno, Liam Brady King*, gabbled the driver, over and over again, *Brady number one*. The brilliance of our Irish leprechaun had been noted.

Although there had been no formal approach, Liam sensed the possibility that Juventus were keen on him. Was it important to put on a good show for them? 'No, it was important I put on a good show for Arsenal,' he emphasises. 'That was first and foremost. I knew if I played well, attention would be drawn. If I was going to leave Arsenal I was going to go to a big club and there was no doubt about it from what I saw in those two or three days that Juventus were a big club.' The thought of Brady making his mark in that elegant Italian city resonated with the family back home in Dublin. For it was in Turin that Liam's Uncle Frank had won his first Irish cap in 1926.

But such thoughts were on hold. One Cup semi-final down, one to go. Arsenal returned to England to resume battle with Liverpool in the FA Cup, bidding to become the first team this century to reach three finals on the spin, and it developed into the longest semi in the history of the competition. Ultimately, Arsenal's season stretched to an unprecedented 70 games, another statistic for the record books. But they would have swapped any of those anorak facts for a trophy. It was too cruel. Arsenal all but mounted two Everests, only to topple over with exhaustion at the point where they could see, but not reach, the zenith. West Ham and Valencia nabbed the silver in the Week from Hell. Two Cup Finals in five days yielded nothing.

'We were tired and the last thing we needed was a boiling hot day at Wembley, being favourites, and West Ham scoring an early goal. They just sat back and we had to work and work and work,' rues Liam. 'In many ways Valencia did the same thing. We didn't have the spark in either game to find the goal that would win us the game. We were by far the better side against Valencia.' Nil-nil, extra-time, penalties, Brady and Rix falter. Graham took the savage blow of failure on his own young shoulders which rendered him inconsolable. The sight of Liam physically dragging him round the lap of honour, forcing him to see that none of the 15,000-strong Arsenal army blamed him for missing the decisive kick, was touching. 'We've been playing the game long enough to know that a penalty's a penalty,' reflects Liam. 'We were hard done by that year. They talk about fixture congestion, we played Saturday against West Ham, Wednesday against Valencia, then we had to go straight to Wolves and Middlesbrough and two wins would put us in the UEFA Cup. We were very professional, we went out against Wolves thinking we still had a chance to salvage something from the season, we beat them, then went to Middlesbrough and we were dead on our feet. 0–5. It was a pretty horrendous week to finish at Arsenal.'

The end. It marked the numbing conclusion of an era which would be filed as undeserving underachievement. So much promise, symbolised not only by the Cup Finals but by the fact that a brilliant Liverpool side couldn't engineer a single win over them in six attempts, and all of it foiled. For post-adolescent Arsenal supporters there was the added gloom of not being allowed to have a childish tantrum, even though it *just wasn't fair*.

For Paul Vaessen, it was the start of a tragic descent. Two years later injury forced him to retire, and he tumbled into the affliction of heroin addiction. Such are the mysteries of life.

For Liam, *la dolce vita* called. Couldn't the club do something to dissuade him? Was there anything that would convince him to stay? Actually, there was. Liam wanted a Championship and had he felt the club was hellbent on winning Division One, he would have postponed his departure. That reassurance was never forthcoming. 'I don't think the ambition was at the club, like it is now,' mulls Liam. 'If that squad could have been strengthened with good players I think we could have won the league. Good players that were commonly known to us, the likes of Mark Lawrenson and Bryan Robson, were coming on the transfer market and Arsenal finished second-best. I think we were interested to a certain amount but when the ante was raised we were out of the race. That disappointed me because if the manager had sat down with me and said, "We're going to win the league, this is the blueprint," I might not have wanted to go abroad. To be fair to Arsenal, it was a period when football wasn't big business, so to spend a lot of money didn't seem to make the sense that it does today. There seems to be a logic in spending it now.

'We proved that we were a very good side in the Cup competitions and I enjoyed those three years at Arsenal where we were the best Cup side in the land. With a couple of players I reckon we could easily have been in the title race. Whereas Liverpool had a squad of 18 very good players, I don't think we had that strength in depth.

'If there was real ambition at the club they would have thought, "Bloody hell, we've got a team and a half here." But the whole thing was let go and didn't recover until George Graham came back. Foresight then was lacking. They should have said, "We want to get the likes of Brady and Stapleton and O'Leary and Rix tied up, really good players who had come through the youth policy, and build on top of that." I think they took us for granted a little bit. Frank's feelings were a bit like mine. Big signings like Malcolm came in and we were left behind a wee bit.

'People said I went for the *lure of the lire* [the words are loaded with sarcasm]. That was a big consideration but if I could maybe have had a compromise on my money here and on top of that been told we were going to win the league . . . but the negotiations I had with Terry Neill weren't going anywhere. I'm a football man; if someone had sat down with me, like a Bill Shankly, and said, "We don't want you to go. We're going to get him and him and have a real crack at the league, then you can go abroad in another three years . . ." it might have been different.' *Che sarà sarà*.

Vaessen was the unfortunate one handed the number 7 shirt for the first post-Chippy match, poor lamb. To the sore eyes in the Highbury audience, no understudy could look the part. It took the club an uncomfortably long time to recover from this mortifying loss, as Rix conceded, the heart was taken out of the team. Not until George Graham returned to rekindle our hopes did we begin to consider the possibility of life after Brady, and even then, for all the wonders George showed us, midfield remained Arsenal's Achilles heel. To be fair to the managers who have failed to replace him, Liam clones hardly come two a penny, nor two a few million quid for that matter.

Way back in the summer of 1971, when Liam arrived at Highbury as an apprentice, he took part in Arsenal's Double parade on the opening day of the new season. The club thought it would be a charming idea to let the youngsters carry the silverware around the pitch to show off to the fans. There, at the front of this gaggle of tracksuited kids, is a scruffy-haired Liam clutching the Championship trophy. At the end of that year he had his hands on the South-East Counties League prize. From that day on, the joys of a red-and-white title eluded him. It's an ironic old game.

When Dennis Bergkamp joined Arsenal he insisted on having the number 10 shirt. On the continent it holds special significance, the number reserved for the player who is the fulcrum of the team. It escaped no Arsenal eye that Liam was Highbury's kingpin, reinforced by Don Howe's admission that his teammates were instructed to give him the ball at every available opportunity. Like Bergkamp today, Brady could play his way out of the most awkward situations with a swift swerve or tender touch. Picture a game against Fenerbahce at Highbury: with half a dozen Turks sandwiching him from all sides, Liam squeezed improbably out of the scrum, even though his most likely escape route seemed to be on a stretcher. The visiting gang were baffled as the soloist ran on with the ball at his feet. A spontaneous standing ovation erupted from all four sides of the ground, even the West Stand Upper, and they take some persuading to shift after a goal. It's a measure of the impression Juventus had of Brady that they bestowed upon him the honour of the number 10.

Liam was Juventus's first foreign signing when Serie A re-opened its frontiers after a 12-year embargo. 'I think they went for Karl-Heinz Rummenigge and Kevin Keegan first, I was a bit down the list,' he smiles, humbly. He wasn't overly concerned about culture shock – having bridged the gulf between Dublin and London, Turin was going to be a piece of *torta* – but what he didn't expect was a traditional Italian reception. Thousands of fans awaited his arrival at the airport and carried him shoulder-high through passport control, officials benignly waving him through. He was immediately thrust into a press conference in front of 40 journalists, and then driven to the training camp to get reacquainted with the team he had beaten only weeks before. When he walked in, a room full of Italian internationals stood up to applaud him, the captain made a welcoming speech and he was expected to respond. It made a change to the halfway house at Highbury. A thorough ego massage? 'Oh, they do it with everybody so I'm not getting carried away,' says Liam, bashfully.

Poignantly, the Championship he always hankered for came in his first season, immediately followed by another. 'I look back with a lot of pleasure on the fact that I won medals in my first two years when a lot of people said I was making a big mistake. *Temperamental Italians, you'll get kicked to death, they are media-obsessive,* that kind of thing.' He shrugs. A dash of piquancy was added when Liam confirmed Juve's second *scudetto* with a penalty. The spot-kick pressure was intensified by the knowledge he would be leaving the club as soon as the season was up, Trappa-toni having decided to replace him with a new foreigner, Michel Platini. All the critics who claimed Liam was too young to take on Serie A at the age of 24 were hushed, and after Juventus he graced the shirts of Sampdoria, Inter Milan and Ascoli. To this day he remains the most successful import from British shores since the days of John Charles and Denis Law.

Liam believes his Italian lessons developed his perspective as well as performance. 'To Italian footballers a career is that: a career. To a player playing in England (although times have changed) only a very small percentage looked beyond the end of the next match let alone the end of the season. Saturday night for me was *How much booze could I get in my system?* and if I was sober by Monday, it would be okay. If I hadn't gone to Italy I probably would have carried on like that. When I went back to West Ham they gave you a fry-up on a Friday, the day before the match, but attitudes have changed and England is not as insular as it used to be. Europe is much smaller now and I think English clubs have cottoned on now to the career side of football, but I learned it 20 years ago. I changed my way of looking at myself.'

It confirmed Don Howe's opinion that Liam's Italian odyssey would be his making. 'I could always sense he wouldn't be at Arsenal for the rest of his life, I knew he needed that next challenge and his trip to Juventus was right for him, to stretch himself.' This didn't stop Howe trying to bring him home when he was manager, and a deal was close before being dashed by financial constraints. From time to time media speculation mooted the possibility of Brady's return, wickedly toying with Arsenal supporters' emotions, like an ex phoning you up out of the blue to tease your fragile sanity. We could hardly blame him for staying – why go back to the girl next door when you can stay with Isabella Rossellini? Why hang out with Lee Chapman and John Hawley and Peter Nicholas when you can kick around with Zico and Socrates and Maradona?

Miserable though Arsenal fans were at missing out on Brady's best days, the club are now reaping the benefits from his experiences. In the summer of 1996, the back pages magnifying every nuance of the Rioch-to-Wenger saga, Arsenal made a crucial acquisition which passed almost unnoticed outside of N5. Red and white phones were nevertheless buzzing: *Chippy's back!* Appointing Brady as Head of Youth Development was a masterstroke. Not only is he brimming with creative ideas, he also embodies the perfect combination of qualities – Arsenal by nurture and European by nature – to impress on the club's future talents.

'When you grow up with a club and you end up playing for them and winning things, you are from that club. I was produced here, I was formulated here. I'd been coming since I was 13, and I only ever wanted to sign for Arsenal. There were other interested clubs but the word spread pretty quickly that I wasn't going to change my mind. I was comfortable with the management, they'd looked after me, and I'm trying to do the very same things at the moment. When we bring boys over from Ireland or other parts of the country, it's important they get to like the club immediately and they say, *When I leave school I would like to come here.* That's what I call the "treatment" I had at Arsenal.

'I wouldn't be interested in this job anywhere else but Highbury. All the teams we had which were successful here, the rock has been the youth policy. I want to get players into the Arsenal team, winning trophies and playing for their country, be it England, Ireland, Scotland or Cameroon. There's ambition in the club now. I don't think this position would have been created otherwise, and that's what sold me the whole thing.' A year into the job, Liam has brought back the stalwart Howe to oversee a revamped coaching set-up, reconstructed the scouting network, set up a programme with a local school which is unlikely to expel pupils for international call-ups, and invited boys from various corners of the globe for trials. And he thinks he might have spotted one or two Irish diamonds.

If you do a double-take at a familiar Dubliner sporting an Italian jacket walking up Avenell Road of a weekday morning, look at that, look at that. 'It's kind of strange walking up Arsenal tube station. I used to do that 25 years ago,' Liam smirks. 'At least I'm my own boss, and if I'm five minutes late I don't get fined now.'

You Little Beauty

KENNY SANSOM

Arsenal 2 Liverpool 1
5 April 1987

Lukic, Anderson, Sansom, Williams, O'Leary, Adams, Rocastle,
Davis, Quinn (Groves), Nicholas, Hayes (Thomas)

Before joining up with England's World Cup squad for Mexico
86, Kenny Sansom bumped into the Millwall manager George
Graham in a wine bar and they chewed the football fat. Too
defensive, thought Kenny of George's methods; too frustrated,
pondered George of Kenny's mental state: this man needs to win
something. The best left-back of his generation had nothing to
show for ten years at the top of his game.

If Sansom reckoned that was frustrating, he hadn't seen nothing yet. His hardship barometer peaked that summer, during
England's quarter-final against Argentina in the Azteca Stadium.
Diego Maradona scored two of the World Cup's most talked-
about goals; one merited superlatives, the other invited ex-
pletives. There is no more grievous feeling in football than being
robbed, and Kenny played in the most shocking swindle the
game has ever known. Mere mention of the fraudster's name
makes his hackles rise to this day: 'Cor, there were some swear
words flying about. He cheated. He cheated us out of a chance
of getting to the World Cup Final. He cheated football. A lot of
people lost a lot of respect for him that day. I did. Steve Hodge
grabbed his shirt – I wouldn't have had that shirt for a million
pounds. Disgraceful. I still think now if ever a game should have

been replayed, that was the one. Looking back, it was one of the worst things to happen to football. The Schumacher foul on Battiston was the worst – he shouldn't have been allowed on a football pitch ever again – but Maradona takes some beating. Horrible.' Kenny hung an enormous photograph of the Hand of God in his home, strategically placed in the lavatory. Now that's an example of how to use your frustration positively.

During that World Cup campaign Kenny discovered Arsenal's new manager was George Graham, a man who would admire Sansom's toilet decor. His managerial philosophy recognised that thwarted ambition, manipulated constructively, could be a power-ful tool for success. Considering the number of unfulfilled souls at Highbury, his appointment could not have come at a more expedient time.

One of Arsenal's foibles is that every decade has its mid-life crisis. A betting man on the mother of all losing streaks could confidently chance his last quid on Arsenal drawing a blank when the year ends in five. All the wonder years since the war have occurred as one decade climbs into another, while the in-between times signal a freefall into the doldrums. So it was High-bury stumbled through one of its nihilistic fazes in the mid-'80s. Flair was undermined by a distinct lack of fire. 'We had some great players and played some great football but we never really punished teams,' Kenny admits. 'With the players we had we should have won more, and any players from that era will tell you the same, because no shadow of a doubt, we had the ability. I suppose we weren't a team of real winners. We settled for playing well instead of saying, "No, we're going to win."' George Graham would see to that. Having drifted through the dreary epicentre of another epoch, he was going to prove to bluesey Arsenal that life begins again in 1986–87.

Kenny's and George's careers had crossed years before at Crystal Palace, when the former was an emerging teenager and the latter was winding down. Kenny soon noticed his new boss had acquired a new ruthlessness. 'We went back a long long way, although I was only a baby then. Everyone remembered George Graham the old Stroller, but when he turned up he was very strict. He had the plan in his mind – most probably written down, knowing George — he stuck to it and it paid off. He's a good judge and he had good luck, and if you can combine the two you're a winner.' The other bonus he had, recalls Kenny, was that he could still strut his stuff on the park. 'He joined in games and showed good ability. That rubs off, you think, *Hang on, he's the best player and he's the manager,* so you try to raise your game to make sure he's not the best next time. George was a good footballer.' The gaffer agrees with this appraisal: 'I had good vision, was a good target-man, exceptional in the air for my height — let's not sit on the fence! My lack of pace was my biggest failure,' he sighs wistfully.

George was prepared to give everyone in the squad he inherited a chance to impress him. There were no wholesale changes and the only new face was raw speed merchant Perry Groves, whom he had been eyeing for Millwall, hardly a signing to trigger a whirl of giddy anticipation. To the critical eyes of the press and the supporters, Graham's early moves suggested anything but the beginnings of a revolution. But away from the limelight, the seeds for a new dawn were being planted in rural Hertfordshire. The players at London Colney were the same but the mood had changed.

George is a great one for sayings, and no sooner was he settled at Highbury than he had one of his favourite quotes printed out and on display to act as a constant inspiration. Penned by the most successful coach in American Football, Vince Lombardi, it cites the three essential elements for winning: technique, discipline and team spirit. With the method of a mathematician and the zest of a speed freak, he set about educating his players in each aspect.

Technique. George demanded an unprecedented level of dedication at the training ground. Particularly if you play in defence. The back four were to be so well drilled they could play with one arm behind their backs (or in the air). He regularly set six attackers on them until they became resistant enough to quell whatever might be thrown at them on a Saturday. 'George had a set routine,' says Kenny, 'He kept doing the things he wanted to do every day, drumming it into everyone so we got an understanding.' Like a scratched record, *clean sheets* was repeated over and over again until it was embedded in the players' brains forever. *Clean sheets, clean sheets,* babbled Viv Anderson to Sansom, O'Leary and Adams as they entered the tunnel every match day.

Discipline. George expected faultless behaviour. Gambling and boozing, those two staple pastimes in the football fraternity, were to be tempered. Not outlawed – he knew better than to try to impose that – but tempered nonetheless. *Remember who you are, what you are, and who you represent* was hammered out, staccato style, like an army chant. On and off the field the players were required to act in a manner which would bring credit to themselves, their family, their profession, Arsenal Football Club, and anyone else who knows them. In the depths of a post-match nightclub, sinking their umpteenth drink, the boys sometimes toasted *Remember who you are, what you are, and who you represent* then fell about laughing. At least the maxim hadn't gone in one ear and out the other.

Team spirit. George advocated togetherness. (Being Frank McLintock's best mate during the Double year, the advantages could not have escaped him.) In order to foster an us-against-the-world mentality, the *us* has to be shatterproof. To create that strength within the camp he removed one or two bad eggs, remotivated a couple of moody egos, and threw his assistant manager Theo Foley into the melting pot. The genial joker who came with George from Millwall was his perfect foil, the jester to provide light entertainment while Graham ruled court. Theo was the butt of much tomfoolery, the buffer if tension arose, and he became an invaluable dressing-room presence. David Rocastle believes without his good-cop to George's bad-cop, Arsenal wouldn't have speeded down Trophy Avenue. 'One glance at Theo would give you a lift, just being his bubbly self, his old Irish eyes smiling. If things weren't going well he would give you that look which said *Look son, don't worry, it'll come good.* He'd put an arm round you and really get you upbeat. If it wasn't for him I don't think we'd have won the Championship in 1989. After we messed up against Derby and Wimbledon, Theo put us in the right frame of mind, he really kept our spirits up. Going into the Anfield game after listening to George and Theo, we felt we could walk on water.'

Foley endeared himself to everyone. Even the Arsenal crowd, to whom he was a perfect stranger, soon warmed to his charms. *Theeeooo-ooo!*, they yelled as he hoofed the ball towards John Lukic in pre-match warm-ups, and in return his beaming smile would light up the stadium. Meanwhile George was plotting and planning and urging and geeing. He commanded discipline and technique while Theo looked after spirit. The three basics were falling nicely into place.

Arsenal's first game under George Graham and Manchester United, Kenny's least favourite team, are in town. It bugs him that they have had a curse on Arsenal in recent years, especially in 1983 when they knocked the Gunners out of both Cups in the semi-finals. 'Any other team and I think we would have won but Man United had this thing over us. I don't like Man United,' he sneers. The season's opener is the perfect opportunity to clean the slate. It finishes 1–0 to the Arsenal, which delights Kenny, and a clean sheet to add to Nicholas's goal pleases the boss. Technique? Looking better already. Discipline? No worries there. Team spirit? We're on the way.

Arsenal soon settle into a rhythm which sees the crowds flock back to Highbury. After some erratic early-season results, the lads embark on a 24-match unbeaten run and climb to the top of the table. Resilience, that quality by which George set so much store, becomes an Arsenal habit. Four undefeated months for a team who hadn't managed more than four undefeated games the previous season is an astounding feat. It all comes to a head at Old Trafford, when Norman Whiteside kicks Arsenal until their nerve snaps. Rocastle is sent off for retaliation and the game degenerates into bitterness. Final score: Manchester United 2 Arsenal 0. Kenny's not happy.

Another trait George encourages is the ability to bounce back, an echo of the defiance of the Double team. Arsenal must rediscover the groove for a Littlewoods Cup semi-final against Tottenham, the most trying test yet for George's starlets. In all honesty, the old enemy have a more rounded team, with Hoddle, Waddle and Ardiles in midfield and Clive Allen scoring goals by the bucketload.

★

Whenever Kenny Sansom and Clive Allen play against each other, age-old gossip is regurgitated. They were the pawns in a transfer swap that stands as one of football's enduring curiosities. Back in the summer of 1980, Arsenal splashed out a club record £1 million for Allen, only to sell him within weeks before he'd ever played a game for the club. Odd. Off he went to Crystal Palace, with goalkeeper Paul Barron, in exchange for Kenny. Very odd. 'Palace wanted Clive Allen and Arsenal wanted myself, two clubs wanted two players,' remarks Kenny. 'It was quite strange that Allen never played a league game for Arsenal. I don't know if there was any messing about.'

Conspiracy theories whistled through football. The truth was buried in the fields of pre-season friendlies, during which Neill realised Allen wasn't in the right mould for Arsenal. He wanted a team player rather than a goal-hanger. There was no doubt Allen was prolific, but Arsenal would have to change their entire system to play to his strengths. Out of an opportunist conversation with Terry Venables, manager at Selhurst Park, the switch was arranged.

Palace had been good for Kenny. The antithesis of a football-crazy kid when he joined up, he was shaped into an international. 'If someone had said to me when I was 12, "You're going to play for England," I would have laughed. *You're joking.* I didn't even know who was in the England team. Football was far from my mind, I was just messing about, going about with the lads doing dares, riding me bike with no hands. I just wanted to go running around the streets and have a laugh, do the things you shouldn't do. Football never entered my mind.' He won his first cap by the time he was 20, and was hailed by his fellow pros as the best left-back in the country, an accolade he went on to receive eight consecutive times.

Consummate professional on the pitch, he remained a scally-wag off it. Kenny had been introduced to the wonders of football wind-ups as a 16-year-old at Crystal Palace. Sitting wide-eyed on the train to Tranmere for his début, Peter Taylor mouthed *I love you* to test out the new kid on the block. Crikey. 'I was a bit gullible,' he mutters. If you don't learn fast in this game you go under. Kenny learned very fast.

He saw the dressing-room as a comedy club as much as an HQ. 'I always messed about. I like a few jokes, tell a few stories. I used to do impressions of Norman Wisdom, Tommy Cooper, Frank Spencer, the simple ones, just for a giggle.' At Highbury he was famous for his mimicry. Did you ever do George Graham, Kenny? 'No, he was too straight-faced. I never did any football players.' Shame, as the squad had its fair share of characters: Anderson the motormouth, Davis the smooth operator, Quinn the gentle giant, Williams the reactionary, and Charlie Nicholas the 1980s-style darling of the North Bank, the laddiest of lads, the prankmeister. 'He nicked David O'Leary's socks for about a year,' Kenny sniggers. 'He just put them in his bag so David had no socks to go home in. He knew it was Charlie but he couldn't catch him – Charlie was too quick.' And psychologists spend years researching group dynamics, analysing how to unite disparate forces.

★

8 February. Tottenham at home. Littlewoods Cup semi-final first leg. Rocastle and Anderson, who have developed a cunning understanding on the right, are both suspended thanks to the animosity of Old Trafford. They are replaced by Groves and Caesar but the team has lost its balance. Allen scores, Arsenal have no answer, and Tottenham swan into the players' lounge preening with the confidence of cockerels who think they are through to Wembley. With a home match to come they had done the hard work, surely.

1 March. Tottenham away. Semi-final second leg. In a White Hart Lane mudbath Allen scores again to make it 2–0 on aggregate, and frankly, the margin should be greater. A creative goal-keeping display from John Lukic sees various parts of his anatomy – anything will do – deny Allen a hat-trick at least by half-time. David Pleat's team feel their final berth is beyond question. Over the corridor George tries to lift the lads. In an act of sporting generosity the Tottenham DJ, whose racket reverberates through to the dressing-room, does his job for him. Over the tannoy his gleeful, mocking voice announces details of Cup Final ticket arrangements, which he caps by playing that sophisticated Chas 'n' Dave number 'Spurs are on their way to Wembley'. 'That just made the lads go berserk! You cheeky so-and-sos!' Kenny exclaims. George is in the middle of his speech and suddenly the place is in chaos. Arsenal roar back onto the pitch, itching to get into Tottenham.

Every Gunner wants the ball. Rocastle and Davis are everywhere, prompting, probing, pushing. Mickey Thomas, in only his second-ever start for the club, is fabulous. Anderson and Sansom fire up the flanks. Tottenham's defence rock on their heels, bewildered by the gangly presence of Quinn and the audacious touch of Nicholas. Throw-in to Arsenal. Rocastle lobs the ball into the box, Quinn flicks on, and there's big Viv Anderson, the leggiest man in football, to poke the ball past Clemence. 'We used to call him "Extension", he had such long legs. You think he ain't gonna get there and all of a sudden his leg just goes again,' says little Kenny admiringly. Arsenal are back in the game and it's a humdinger. The pace is frantic, and Rocastle speeds down the right to deliver a cross into the path of Quinn, who releases all that half-time venom by ramming the ball into the net. Arsenal go ballistic. Tottenham wobble. Spurs aren't on their way to Wembley yet.

Extra-time produces chances but no more goals. Pleat wins the toss for the replay venue, so hostilities will resume at White Hart Lane on Wednesday night. George indulges in a touch of kidology. It augurs well, he reckons, because Arsenal have won twice at Tottenham and failed to beat them in two meetings at Highbury. 'I always enjoyed playing at Spurs!' adds Kenny.

4 March. Tottenham away. Semi-final second-leg replay. Arsenal's skipper stops his car on the way to the game to buy some champagne. 'I thought *We're gonna win this* so I bought a magnum,' says Kenny. An hour into the game and there's no way of telling whether that was a good hunch or the kiss of death. The tension is unbearable. It's 0–0 for ages and the longer the game goes on, the more everyone feels one goal will win it. Fifteen minutes to go. Allen, who hasn't had a kick all game apart from a cynical two-footed lunge on Davis, pounces: 1–0 to Tottenham. 'Apart from Ian Wright nowadays, I think Clive Allen was the best finisher I've ever seen,' Kenny admits. Arsenal are immediately knocked by a second blow as Nicholas is carried off with a damaged ankle, and on comes Ian Allinson, the definitive squad player. Somehow, Arsenal have to muster all that resilience and defiance that George has been banging on about all season. Eight minutes to go. Davis hooks a long pass deep into Tottenham territory and Allinson chases, but the ball won't drop for him. He's in the box, shoot for God's sake, shoot! He can't – the ball still hangs in the air. Eventually it comes to ground and Allinson squeezes it between a tiny gap at the near post: 1–1. The unsung substitute wears a madman's grin.

Like a surge of electricity, the joy of the comeback sparks Arsenal and conversely saps Tottenham. It's clear who's in the ascendancy as extra-time approaches. In injury time O'Leary stands over a free-kick on the halfway line. Rocastle picks up the story. 'It was a long punt up the field – not the typical Arsenal style. The ball goes to old wooden-head Ian Allinson on the edge of the area. I don't know what he was doing trying to shoot from there, but anyway, the ball ricochets to me and I know I have to get a good touch before I swing my left foot because it's non-existent. I see it go under Ray Clemence's body right in front of the Arsenal fans who are going absolutely berserk. I turn round and all I can see is Michael jumping on top of me, then Paul, then Viv, then the whole team. I was trying to breathe, actually.

'I always remember David Pleat's face crumpled when the goal went in. You notice these little things. I looked at Gary Stevens and he was looking up at the clock to see how long to go. What a feeling when the ref blew the whistle, to know I was in my first Cup Final, Arsenal's first Cup Final for years, against Liverpool. We ran to the Arsenal fans and this big long-haired guy who looked like he was straight out of Bodie and Doyle ran on the pitch and threw his arms around me.'

The entire Arsenal family, together, savour the moment in a collective embrace. Everyone, from George Graham in his lucky red scarf to the injured Steve Williams to Perry Groves who wasn't picked to Kevin Campbell of the youth team to Gary Lewin the physio, everyone is on the pitch hugging and pogo-ing in front of all the hugging, pogo-ing fans. 'When we won and went up to them they were going absolutely mental, they were like caged lions,' says Kenny. 'We were going berserk too. That was our season. From the fans' point of view, if you beat Tottenham twice it don't matter if you finish mid-table. As long as you beat Spurs. It meant so much to the fans and their passion catches you. You just *know*.' Pleat tried manfully to be philosophical. 'People died tonight in hospitals,' he meditated on *Midweek Sport Special*. The Gooners, blissfully oblivious, danced down the High Road singing '*One-nil down, two-one up, we knocked Tottenham out the Cup*.' It was a leitmotif that would serve Arsenal well.

The celebrations were only just beginning. 'When we won, the chairman and vice-chairman bought two crates of champagne in so I thought I'd keep the magnum to myself,' laughs Kenny. 'A lot of us had a lot to drink. The next day I had to go to Birmingham in the morning for *Pebble Mill at One* to talk about the game and I was a bit the worse for wear.' Sansom, who was teetotal when he joined the club, was now a fully fledged member of football's drinking and gambling set. 'I never touched a drop of alcohol until I was 21. I didn't like it, wasn't interested in it. Me and my wife didn't go to pubs so we used to go to bingo or the pictures – we used to get some stick off the lads but we enjoyed it so we didn't mind. Then the lads start going down the pub, I joined in and away it went. I don't know if it's a good thing or a bad thing. It's good for camaraderie and all the lads got on really well. A few games of snooker, a few beers – sometimes too many.

'I gambled every day. It was one of those things. I didn't gamble with me life, I didn't gamble all my money but I gambled. Some played snooker, some played golf, some went down the gym; I enjoyed gambling. Watching the horses or the dogs, having a bit of a bet, winning a couple of quid. All buzzes are different and I enjoyed it. Now I don't bother going in betting shops but I do watch. If we've got some people round of an afternoon we just have a pound on the first past the post. It's a giggle.'

But that season his fluttering ways far exceeded the limits of the odd pound. Kenny's afternoon entertainment hit the tabloids and the club had to step in to help him to control his income. Did it ever affect your career, Kenny? 'If you lose money or do something silly it does affect you and the way you perform. I imagine it affected me a little bit on a Saturday but I didn't realise at the time. That little slight edge can be the difference between getting 100 caps and getting 86 caps.'

On the subject of players whose outside interests diminish their brilliance, Charlie Nicholas was the maestro. Talent-wise, he was a rare bird (and he was partial to them, too). Arsenal's Bonnie Prince sought beauty on and off the pitch, only it was easier to find away from Highbury. At times he was a parody of the footballing wonder he should have been. Charlie's relationship with Arsenal was like a blind date that should have been perfect yet never quite worked out; when he signed in 1983 the club was crying out for a hero and the player was eager for a stimulating challenge. Still, even if he didn't score the 50 goals a season he'd notched at Celtic, everyone had a soft spot for him. He may not have inhabited the stellar world of Alex James or Liam Brady or Ian Wright, but he sparkled more than most.

George Graham, so the saying went, didn't like stars. The manager scoffs at such a generalisation. Admittedly he isn't enamoured by flickering stars, but the strong stars, the ones who shine all year round, he finds very agreeable. *Performing stars,* he called them, bigshots who were big on motivation. Liverpool, he lauded, had a whole constellation of them.

George Graham's aim was to build a dynasty at Arsenal, emulating the philosophy of the 1930s dominators, and more recently, of Liverpool. They were the club who for two decades appeared to have winning written into their constitution. If Arsenal had been underdogs against Tottenham in the semi-final, compared to their opponents in the Littlewoods Cup Final they were mere pups. The Liverpool of Hansen, Lawrenson, Whelan, Molby, Rush and McMahon oozed superiority; they were holders of the 1986 Double, had won the competition four times in the '80s, and had beaten Arsenal home and away in the league. 'Liverpool had the edge,' states Kenny, 'and I think they thought that themselves.'

In Ian Rush they had the most potent weapon in the English game. His presence intimidated teams, not only because he was the supreme goalscorer of the era, but also due to the knowledge that Liverpool never lost a game in which he scored, and that awesome trait ran for an astonishing 145 matches. Arsenal, considered the pundits, may as well enjoy the day because the only thing they will take away from Wembley is memories.

George's plan is to compress the midfield, to hound Molby and McMahon so they don't have time to manipulate one of those classic breaks which serve Rush so well. Perhaps it's the glow of a sundrenched Wembley, the thrill of the 100,000 throng but the lads take a while to settle (Liverpool might be blasé about it but it's a new buzz for most of the Arsenal boys). A swift incisive move cuts straight through Arsenal's midriff, just what George was wary of, and there's Rush, the harbinger of doom, to finish.

'*We can't win*,' thinks Kenny. '*Whenever he scores Liverpool never lose* . . . Then all of a sudden the game just turns round, we seem to have more of the ball, just get on top of them. We seem to be more determined – maybe we want it more.' Within five minutes of the goal Arsenal have a free-kick on the edge of the box, dead centre. Davis strikes . . . it hits the wall, Sansom floats the ball in, Anderson crosses, Adams shoots . . . it's blocked, Nicholas tries . . . it hits the post, Anderson crosses again, Nicholas tries again . . . it's in! The goal was clearly meticulously planned at Colney, designed to outmanoeuvre refined Liverpool. It's a shambolic scramble but who cares? Team spirit? Fantastic. Discipline? Superb. Technique? What the hell.

Ten minutes remain and both teams prepare their substitutes for a late assault. It's representative of the gulf between the two teams that Liverpool bring on Kenny Dalglish, megastar, and Arsenal introduce Perry Groves, mega-enthusiast. Dalglish barely touches the ball. Groves, however, latches on to a pass from Sansom and skips gaily past Gillespie, pulls the ball back to Nicholas, and if the first goal was unorthodox, the second was similarly bizarre. Charlie's shot takes an extreme diversion via a Liverpool leg and trickles past Grobbelaar in super slow motion. One-nil down, two-one up. Twice in the semi-final and now again in the final. 'Charlie went berserk,' smirks Kenny. 'He didn't have the best of times down here but when he scored that goal it was like heaven for him. All our mouths went dry, like we've actually done it. When that goal went in, that was that. Game over.'

Another man who is unconstrained is Bob Wilson, sitting behind the goal-line unable to contain his glee. Echoes of the 1971 FA Cup Final vibrate, one-nil down, two-one up against Liverpool and a Charlie with the winner. Crucially, Ian Rush has no response. For the first time in six years, he scores and Liverpool lose. The Arsenal boys skip about shouting '*You Little Beauty!*' another of George Graham's favourite sayings. 'I've maybe got four or five big thrills of my career and that was one of them,' says Kenny. 'On the way up to the Royal Box someone gave me a silly hat and I got so much stick for wearing it as I picked up the trophy but I didn't care what I did. If someone had asked me to shave me head I'd have done it at the time.'

The press scrawled their Champagne Charlie stories, for all the right reasons for once. They were used to reproaching a talent dimmed by the bright lights of London. Liverpool, they opined, the team he turned down to join Arsenal, would have been a better option (Charlie now admits they were probably right). And he wasn't the only Arsenal player who might have won a cabinet full of medals on Merseyside. In 1980, ten minutes after Kenny signed for Arsenal, Bob Paisley phoned the Sansom household to invite him to Anfield. 'Liverpool then were the best club side England will ever see, without doubt. They were the tops. I could have signed for Liverpool but it was too late. You never know what's going to happen.' For that afternoon at Wembley at least, musings on what might have been were obliterated by triumph.

★

Captain Kenny eventually had his hands on the silver which reflects success. 'Not many people have had the honour of being captain of Arsenal,' he says. 'I'm a good talker on the pitch and I try and help everyone but, to be fair, I'd rather be a player and leave the other responsibilities to someone else. Dave O'Leary was a good captain and I'd like to have seen Graham Rix do the job on a more permanent basis. I learned a lot from Graham even though he was only a year older than me. He was at the club a long time – he'd have been a superb captain for Arsenal.' Sansom, Rix, O'Leary and Anderson were the experienced heads in George's first year. In the close-season Viv left to line his pockets at Manchester United and the funboys Kenny and Graham were soon fazed out of the manager's plans. David, one of Highbury's greatest loyalists, remained a trusted steed until his legs could carry him no more. The relative fates of the senior brigade were symbolic. George wanted total dedication to the cause – if money was the motivation, or if you enjoyed life off the field too excessively for his liking, you were on your way.

'When Viv left it snowballed,' reflects Kenny. 'It was obvious the older players were going to go. I didn't think so at the time but, looking back, you can see George wanted to make his own team. Everyone built it up as a big split but all he did was get the players out who weren't doing it. He was saying *If you're not going to perform, you're going to be in the reserves.* He was right. I don't think it was personal. When you're a player you think *He's dropped me so he doesn't like me.* That's an easy get-out but it wasn't true. He was trying to send me a message and I didn't take it on board; he wanted improvement so he made decisions. That's all it was. He did it the way he thought was right and he was right because he won two Championships and a load of Cups.'

Kenny was sold in the season George's new Arsenal took on Liverpool for a more prestigious trophy – the Championship. He returned to Highbury with Newcastle, for a match Arsenal won 1–0. He scored a perfectly good goal which the referee dis-allowed. Strange how things work out in football. His enduring memory from that day was the reaction from the crowd. Kenny's mum, who always came to Highbury to watch her boy, gave the game a miss because she worried he might be tormented. 'I went back there and I was like a God,' he says. 'The fans from every side were singing. Thanks. They say you don't realise how good the club is until you go back there and I do now.'

Kenny was on holiday in Cyprus the night Arsenal won the

league at Anfield. 'I thought, "Bloody hell, I could have been part of that." It done me a little bit, felt like a bit of a kick in the teeth but I was pleased for the lads. They were a good bunch and they worked for each other.' George had constructed a new back line in the sweatshop of London Colney – Winterburn, Dixon and Bould were the new cogs in an Arsenal defensive mechanism which was guaranteed to purr for a long time to come. They linked up with the masterful Adams, who took over from Kenny as captain, and O'Leary, the only old-head George kept on board. While Kenny enjoyed a balmy Mediterranean evening, David bawled his eyes out on the pitch at Anfield. The only one of the Dublin three to sign and stay when Brady and Stapleton departed for bigger contracts, he was an Arsenal champion at last.

Technique, discipline, team spirit. That was the night when the three magic ingredients blended to achieve the ultimate. That was the night the team that George built became legend. And there was plenty more to come.

Blood Brothers

DAVID ROCASTLE

Manchester United 0 Arsenal 1
20 October 1990

Seaman, Dixon, Winterburn, Thomas, Bould, Adams, Rocastle,
Davis, Smith, Merson, Limpar

Supporters like to believe they can affect the outcome of a game, playing the so-called '12th man' who can suck the ball into the net, or, occasionally, suck it into the crowd. This explains why the North Bank is a mass of mayhem screaming *MIIISSSS!* at the poor bloke about to take a penalty for the opposition. Fifteen thousand crammed into the terrace wave their arms about like voodoo dancers invoking the power to put him off. It's the last minute of an FA Cup tie and Arsenal are leading 2–1. All eyes on Manchester United's Brian McClair. If he converts it, it'll mean a replay at Old Trafford; if he misses, the Gunners are through. He looks a little nervy, steps up, then hoofs the ball gloriously into the middle of the terrace. The 12th men are beside themselves with glee. McClair, head bowed, makes that lonely walk away from the penalty spot. Nigel Winterburn saunters over to have a few quiet words with the beleaguered striker. They are not of a consoling nature. Thus was a simmering feud born.

A warm frisson was par for the course when George Graham's Arsenal met Alex Ferguson's Manchester United. We had already witnessed David Rocastle's red mist and red card in 1987 (that his adversary Whiteside was let off the hook only added to the acrimony). Then came the McClair–Winterburn enmity in

1988. Next up Tony Adams's own-goal and the subsequent brutal donkey baiting in 1989. These were but pinpricks compared to the needle which jabbed so deep in 1990.

21 October. Man United away. Like all the recent encounters between the two clubs, this one has an abrasive texture, a capacity to sting. From the off the tempo is agitated, highly charged, perpetual motion. Every 50-50 challenge is full blooded and the tone is set: if you go in, you go in committed. The roaring crowd warm to the theme; it might not be elegant but it's enthralling stuff.

There's nothing quite like a goal to stir up the frenzy, especially if it is spiced by controversy. Just before half-time Arsenal, against the run of play, force a corner. Anders Limpar bolts towards the flag to take it short, then whips in a shot from an angle so acute it takes everyone by surprise, including goalkeeper Les Sealey. He falls into his goalmouth and scoops the ball back into play but referee Keith Hackett, in the perfect position to judge whether it crossed the line, signals a goal without hesitation. Sealey is furious, Ferguson seethes, the United fans voice their incensed discontent. Old Trafford is stewing nicely.

When a game is played on the very edge of control, at the boundary of passion, there is always a chance the protagonists might topple over to the other side. That's not sport, that's life. It's human emotion, spontaneous reaction. It's road rage, or bar-room barneys, or family fall-outs at Christmas. Rationality takes a back seat, and all it takes for nagging tension to spill into aggression is the flick of a switch.

On the hour tempers suddenly escalate. A vendetta brews between Limpar and Denis Irwin: Anders trips the United full-back, who responds by taking a sly kick while the winger is on the ground. The Swede offers to shake hands, only for Irwin to angrily brush his conciliatory gesture off. Here's the rub. This all happens right under Winterburn's nose. Nigel glowers. He sees it as his business to support Anders, a fragile little fellow new to the English game, and tells Irwin in no uncertain terms he finds that kind of behaviour unacceptable. Hackett wags a finger at the United man but it's Nigel's finger which lingers on the switch.

From the restart the ball pings between Winterburn, McClair,

Irwin and Limpar, not your ideal quartet to be instantly embroiled in the action. The two Red Devils sandwich Anders and Nigel lunges in like a man possessed, a tackle so late it should have been registered the following week. Flick. Temperature overload. Meltdown. McClair piles into Winterburn, booting him in the back as he lies prostrate, and the boys come steaming in. David Rocastle is one of the first on the scene. 'Something happened, I didn't even know what it was, but all I saw was a few of my team-mates in trouble,' he says, 'and if you see your team-mates in trouble, you go in, within the laws of the game, to try and help them out. It was nothing malicious towards Man United players but it was our team-mate, our little blood brother, in trouble. They were kicking Nigel in on the floor like a night-club brawl. That's what got us upset. If it was just a bad tackle, you wouldn't go in like that, no chance. But when I saw them kicking into Nigel I ran over, thinking, *You can't have this!* It just epitomised Arsenal's team spirit. We went in there and we stuck up for each other. At Arsenal we never, ever started any brawls – we just finished them.'

Limpar lands a quick strike then hurtles down the touchline with Ince and Bruce in hot pursuit; Thomas and Davis seek retribution on McClair; Sealey has Rocastle in an armlock; Adams and Pallister act as peacemakers; Smith watches it all from a safe distance with a look of dismay . . . It's mayhem right in front of the dug-outs and both managers and all the staff and subs try desperately to restore order.

Handbags at ten paces emerges as the stock description and it's all over in 30 seconds. Poor Keith Hackett has to settle the mess, which he does by booking Winterburn and Limpar, who are booed to the rafters every time they touch the ball for the remainder of the game. Irwin and McClair, the other two major miscreants, get away scot-free. Arguably, probably, all four should have walked.

Old Trafford rattles with noise as the molten heat of the drama permeates into the stands. Somehow the players must cool themselves to see out the match, and all 22 settle to serve up a pulsating half-hour of football. Still committed, still competitive, still searching for goals, but no more argy-bargy. For some reason, few notice that it turns into a thrilling game. It wouldn't have mattered if it finished 10–9, the story had been written.

So, Arsenal gain three well-earned points at a traditionally unlucky ground, but pleasure is diluted by the knowledge that Limpar's goal will not be the moment replayed on the *News at Ten* and headlined in Sunday's papers. The media are appalled by 'The Battle of Old Trafford'. Reports are damning, and since this is not the first time the men from Highbury have leaned towards the seamier side of the game (a fracas with Norwich the previous season sprang to mind) Arsenal are portrayed as football's forces of evil.

Rocky remembers how the Gunners were expected to beat a hasty retreat from Lancashire, eyes down and tails between legs. Not so. 'People thought we would be going onto the bus straight away but we went into the Man United players' lounge and held our heads up high. I think a lot of rival managers, including Alex Ferguson, admired that team spirit we had and thought they should instil some of that in their own teams. No one can condone a big punch-up in the middle of the field but in the heat of the moment, these things arise. The punch-ups in rugby are ten times worse but perceived as part and parcel of the game. In football it's the biggest sin ever and they want to lock you up. We all knew people were after Arsenal, they made us out to be villains of the piece, especially as we were on probation after the Norwich incident.' Spurred by a national outcry, and ashamed by the fact the game had been broadcast in 64 countries, the Football Association immediately charged Arsenal and Manchester United with bringing the game into disrepute. The matter of how best to punish two of the nation's most powerful clubs becomes a *cause célèbre*. Some want to see £1 million fines imposed, some suggest they be thrown out the FA Cup, some call for bans, points deductions, or even relegation. The hullabaloo spawns such hyperbole, it's surprising nobody demands public flogging.

The FA is under immense pressure to kick both clubs *IN THE BRAWLS* (courtesy of *The Sun*) and Arsenal attempt to assuage the damage by taking a hard line from within. Winterburn, Limpar, Davis, Thomas and Rocastle are each docked two weeks'

PROUD TO SAY THAT NAME

wages and George Graham accepts a £10,000 fine. 'I felt a bit aggrieved,' reflects Rocky. 'I didn't think I'd done a lot to be fined. I was going in for a team-mate in need and I didn't even do anything. Les Sealey had his big goalie arms around me, I couldn't get out anyway. I was most upset he was squashing me.' (Later, in the tunnel, David explained to Sealey he didn't take to being squashed.)

Highbury's in-house financial penalties cut no ice with the FA. Both clubs are ordered to pay £50,000 and Arsenal forced to forfeit two points and United one. As the two wealthiest football institutions in the country the money is tolerable, but as teams chasing the title, points deducted is calamitous. North London is in uproar. The three points won at Old Trafford are now one; the six-point lead Liverpool set in the Championship is now eight.

On decision day, David went to see a show to escape the clamour. As he left the theatre an Arsenal fan broke the news. *Can you believe what they've done to us?* the Gooner gulped miserably, *The league's gone now.* 'This guy was really upset,' remembers Rocky. 'I thought, bloody hell, they've obviously found us the guilty party, which upset me more than the two points because you can always make them up. Us being deducted two to Man United's one was saying that we were the trouble-makers. We weren't proud of the actions we took and because you're footballers you have to be so much more disciplined but if you see a mate on the street you react. It was difficult to accept.

'Our spirit held us in good stead. The media was against us and we had a responsibility to avoid putting the club in even more dire straits. Millwall might have had the song "No one likes us, we don't care", but I think that was appropriate for Arsenal. What they couldn't do was destroy our team spirit. I thought we had the best players to win the title in those days anyway but there was no one who had team spirit like ours. We'd been slaughtered in more ways than one and the only way to show our resilience was to stay together and get the points to win the Championship. It never crossed our minds that we'd blown it. The immediate reaction was to do it for ourselves.'

★

The Old Trafford brawl is the game which shapes Arsenal's season. The siege mentality is bolstered and the punishment serves as a permanent incentive to conquer the First Division. They respond to the points deduction the only way they know how: by unleashing their frustration on the next team to come their way. Arsenal 4 Southampton 0.

Although the high drama of Anfield in 1989 could never be matched, the title challenge of 1991 is coloured with theatrical twists. Two years before, the volcanic explosion came right at the end and this time the season unfolds with optimum intensity rumbling throughout. Try as they might to get on with the football, the club unwittingly manufactures paper bullets which are fired relentlessly at the Marble Halls by a press George Graham describes as *hostile*. The players metaphorically fit themselves with steel vests to absorb the flak.

The next game at Loftus Road is marked not only by a scintillating comeback – one-nil down becomes three-one up in the last 12 minutes – but also by the obligatory 'scandal' which shadows Arsenal's every move. Tony Adams, who had been pummelled by a verbal tirade all game, is censured for flicking V-signs at the section of QPR fans who had reviled him.

The pace of events is breathless. Four days later, partners in crime Manchester United come to Highbury and destroy Arsenal in the League Cup. The meanest of defences, which had been breached only six times in the first four months of the season, concede as many in one game. 2–6, a debilitating scoreline. George reminds his shellshocked troops of the 0–5 battering Arsenal took from Stoke in the Double year. Dig in, he urges, use it.

They do, cruising past Liverpool 3–0 in their next outing at Highbury four days on. In spite of the points deduction, Arsenal are now hot on Merseyside heels, only three points the difference. Even so, the result is tinged with bad blood – Liverpool accuse Limpar of diving to con the referee into awarding a penalty. Arguments rage. For the tabloids football is a sideshow as far as Arsenal are concerned. 'People couldn't come to terms with the fact we were resilient,' Rocky believes. 'Our resilience was second to none and that's what got us through some hard times to win the Championship. For some reason people didn't like that. Maybe it's the club's profile. George used to make a point of it, every time we had a problem he told us we should rise above it and it would make us stronger.'

With each new subplot the club pulls closer together, augmenting the gulf between us and the outside world. We have to stay unified, because the way things are going everyone is entitled to wonder *Whatever next?* The microscopic eye of the media sharpens its focus on Highbury, waiting for another impropriety . . . 19 December, just in time for Christmas, Tony Adams is imprisoned for drink driving.

'That was devastating,' recalls Rocky. 'I had just recovered from a broken toe and was on the coach back from a reserve game against Fulham. It came on the news that Tony had been jailed and I went stone cold. I thought, *Something must be wrong, they couldn't have* . To be honest we didn't think he would be sent down. We thought he might get community service but, because of the time of year, they obviously wanted to make an example of him. It was our Christmas party that night. We were supposed to be meeting up in Islington to go on our boys night out and everyone was in sombre mood. All we could think about was Tony. We don't condone what he did but he made a mistake. He didn't kill or hurt anyone. He's a normal human being and if he wasn't Tony Adams the Arsenal footballer maybe he wouldn't have gone to prison. We were dumbstruck. The boys thought Tony wouldn't want us to be moping around, the kind of character he is, he would want us to carry on the night. We did but it was half-hearted and subdued, people sitting around talking, trying to find out how we could go to see him and write him letters.

'Nobody really appreciates what he went through, and to come back even stronger and achieve what he has, captaining England in the European Championships, that's the Tony we've always loved. Not many players would have been able to cope. Tony being Tony, he thought he committed the crime so he'd do the time. That's how he is. The hardest part, which really hurt Tony, was the donkey chants. There aren't too many people calling him a donkey now, are there? For someone who has grown up with Tony, I've seen what he has had to take. No footballer should have to take what Tony Adams went through. He used to come out the tunnel and a load of carrots were lobbed at him. Every time he touched the ball, *EE-AW*. As a footballer and as a man, nobody should be subjected to that.'

Was there a sense of let's win the league for Tony? 'The Arsenal way is to get on with business as usual. The Arsenal way is never to mope around,' Rocky explains. 'The club have gone through a lot in the last few years. We never showed our emotions in public and that's what made us grow up as men. We tried to keep it in perspective. Contrasting football with taking your civil liberties away from you makes you put things into proportion. We still had to go and do a job for ourselves and the Arsenal people. It became another skin on our backs, another thing for us to cope with. We coped with it unbelievably well.'

What about you, Tony? Would you have felt you let the side down if they couldn't win the league without you? 'I think they'd won it by the time I got out of Chelmsford nick,' he smiles, 'They were well on the way, that's for sure.'

★

Close the Pandora's box for a moment. Look, without prejudice, without distraction, at the simple fact of Arsenal's season 1990–91. George's boys came closer than any team this century to invincibility. Throughout the league campaign they were beaten only once, and in that game at Stamford Bridge David Hillier played as an emergency centre-back after Steve Bould, who assumed man-mountain stature in Adams's absence, hobbled off crocked at half-time, which says it all. Historians point to Preston's unbeaten season in 1888–89, but the league only comprised 22 games then, and Arsenal's single defeat, incidentally, didn't come until their 24th match. Makes you think. Now peek inside the Pandora's box and realise this golden year was achieved against a turbulent backdrop; two points deducted, two months without the captain, too many slings and arrows for most teams to take. Arsenal had stronger spirit than Smirnoff.

For Seaman, Linighan and Limpar it was one hell of an introduction to Highbury life. Especially as the seven-figure transfer fees commanded by the new goalkeeper, centre-half and winger were questioned initially, the critics wailing that there was nothing wrong with Johnny Lukic, worrying about George's obsession for collecting central-defenders, and wondering who this little Swedish guy was.

Seaman proved his eminence from day one, and surely no other goalkeeper has enjoyed such an immense début season – his 24 clean sheets and 18 goals conceded stands as a club record. Linighan faced the unenviable task of deputising for Adams during his Christmas break, which he undertook boldly. And Limpar was the magician, the matchwinner. 'When we signed him from Cremonese in Serie B nobody had heard of him, which is startling, and he was absolutely brilliant,' George enthuses. 'Anders' first six months was the main reason we won the Championship. He was sensational.'

Freshers were quickly assimilated into the fold, says Rocastle. 'It blended because of the types of personality they were. We never had anyone who thought they were too big for their boots, we never had anyone who thought they were the star of the team. The boys that came in were always one of the boys as long as they gave 100 per cent on the pitch. We all got on well together – I wouldn't say we were all bosom buddies going out all the time – but once a month we'd all go out as a team on a boys night out to get the camaraderie going.' That old chestnut about camaraderie, a recurring theme from Double days through Cup Finals to Anfield. You couldn't keep this lot down if you gave them lead boots.

How did the lads react to that capitulation at Chelsea? Arsenal 4 Crystal Palace 0. And there was one more bodyblow to hit the team during 1991 – the North London FA Cup semi-final at Wembley. Brave talk of another Double was silenced. In the most gruesome way imaginable to anyone of a red and white persuasion. A Gunner with a penchant for self-mutilation could not have felt such torture. Mercifully, the team provided the perfect antidote, sticking steadfastly to their Championship course.

Poetically, Arsenal arrived at their title destiny on a night they hosted Manchester United. The fixture computer that year had a nice line in black humour: the side who clashed with the Gunners at Old Trafford, who crushed Arsenal 6–2 at Highbury, who

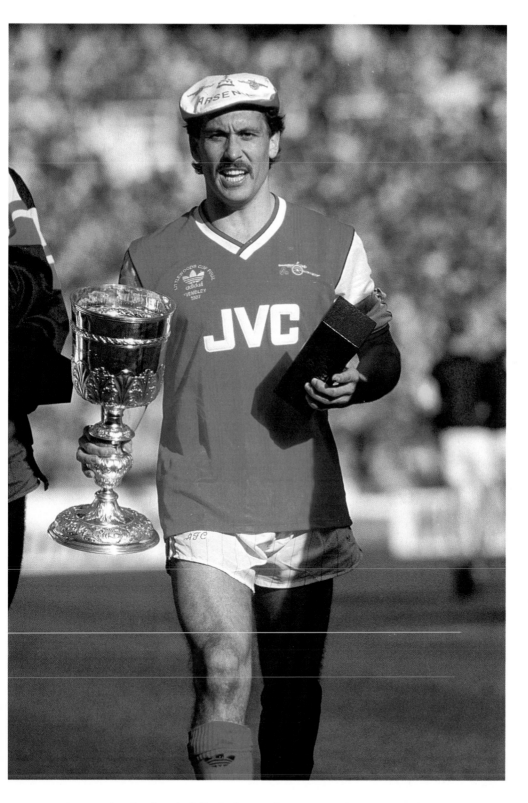

Kenny Sansom has his hands full of silver and George Graham's Arsenal start as they mean to go on

George's finest hour. It was up for grabs at Anfield, Mickey Thomas grabbed it, and the old Stroller becomes the Messiah

David Rocastle bleeds Arsenal

Tony Adams – always a colossus

Saluting another last-gasp winner to bring the Cup Double to Arsenal

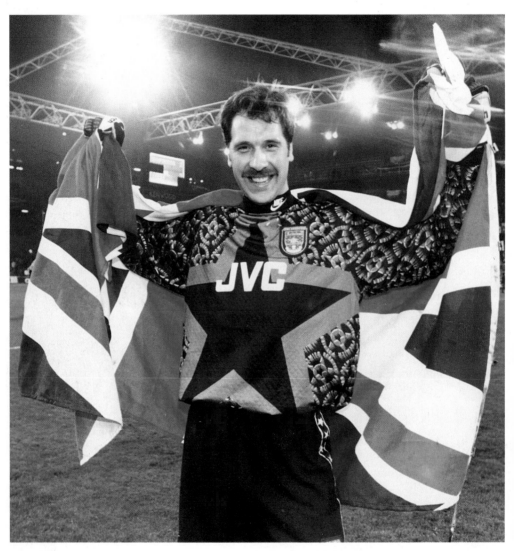

Arsenal's and England's Number One

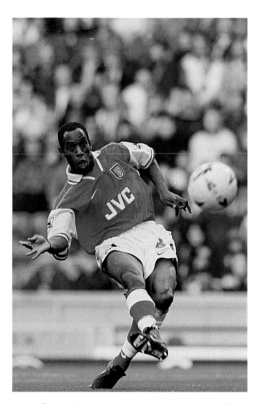

The fire and the ice: Ian and Dennis go for goal. It's a love thing after beating Tottenham 3–1

Symbols of the present glance into the future

provided the two momentous matches which fuelled Arsenal's sense of purpose, they were the side who lined up to clap the new English Champions onto the field. Neat.

Graham's second title couldn't have offered a greater contrast to his first. It was won with two games to spare and his team didn't even have to kick a ball in anger to claim the trophy as Nottingham Forest beat Liverpool during the afternoon to end Merseyside hopes. Gooners hooked to trannies in the streets of N5 and squinting at televisions in the teeming pubs started to party. The foundations of the Plimsoll Arms on St Thomas's Road buckled when Steve McMahon's face filled the screen with a minute to go. Meanwhile the team stood awkwardly in the players' tunnel being filmed as they watched the final whistle from the City Ground on TV monitors. 'It was a bit of an anti-climax but also a relief because nobody wanted it to go to the last game again,' remembers Alan Smith. No such reserve for the fans. Proud, loud and fired by defiance, they cherished the moment to the full: *You can stick your fucking two points up your arse!* was number one on the Arsenal hit parade.

Smudger netted a hat-trick to take him towards his second Golden Boot as United were defeated 3–1. The irony may have escaped certain sections of the media but that night, the football was a mere sideshow for Arsenal. Something sitting off the field, namely a piece of silverware waiting to be presented, was at the forefront of everyone's minds. A flag as big as a house which had travelled to terraces all over the country bearing the legend *This is Arsenal* was unfurled from the Clock End boxes, embellished with two new words. *The Champions.* To cap it all Arsenal displayed all their finery on the last day of the season with a 6–1 rout of Coventry. Limpar's dancing feet made goalkeeper Ogrizovic dizzy and the Super Swede saluted his first season with a trio of fancy goals. This team with the infamous defence could score a few as well.

'Everyone called us a long-ball team,' says Rocky, 'but we played horses for courses. If we played a physical team who tried to outbattle us we'd knock the ball up to Alan Smith who was probably one of the best players at holding the ball up and take it from there. When we played teams who wanted to play an intricate passing game we had players of the calibre of Paul Davis, Michael Thomas, myself, Paul Merson, Anders Limpar. You couldn't call those players long-ball merchants.' The 1991 celebrations were a strange time for David, who had missed the second half of the season after breaking a toe on Boxing Day and was struggling to return to the side. 'I didn't really feel part of it. Compared to 1989 the difference in feeling was extreme.'

Another man who was struck by the distinction was Tony Adams. 'Because of the way we did it at Anfield I think it was important for everyone to see how damn good we were,' smiles the captain. 'To do it in style, to do it with class, to lose once that season when I was in bloody prison – they can't even go a game without me – to be fair Steve Bould came off that game too. He was fabulous that year. Dave Seaman and Bouldy were absolutely instrumental in winning that season. And Alan Smith. *Ooh, fantastic . . .*' He begins to gush.

It has been known for Arsenal and Manchester United to contest a game without the slightest niggle. One such occasion occurred when the Red Devils turned out for David O'Leary's farewell match in 1993. The mood was so jovial they even gave the 20-year career man a goal. To pave the way for this miracle their defence parted biblically, three times, before he could hit the target. The Arsenal faithful cheered United's generous sportsmanship. This great game of ours continues to surprise. One man who enjoyed the night almost as much as O'Leary was David Rocastle, then at Leeds, who made a guest appearance. He was so eager to play for Arsenal again he turned up two hours before anyone else and sat on his favourite treatment table in the dressing-room wearing his red-and-white shirt and a grin the size of the North Bank. He felt utterly forlorn when he was sold but his passion remains undiminished, and his glittering Highbury days abide in the memory. Players often claim they have a club in their heart but when Rocky talks about Arsenal he is only one step away from infatuation. 'He loved Arsenal and he still does,' enthuses Ian Wright. 'Loves them.'

The roots of his affection were planted when he was a boy.

Highbury was his home from home. The feeling of being part of the team, part of the Marble Hall community, attracted him like a magnet. David's father died when he was five and at the club he found an atmosphere in which people guided him, encouraged him, had time for him. 'I never had a father figure coming to watch his kid play,' he says. 'My mum would have loved to have come but there were three other kids and I was the oldest. She gave me support mentally even though she couldn't give it physically at the games. I'd be turning up on my own and I think it did make me strong.

'As apprentices we virtually lived together. Even though we weren't in the same digs we lived in and out of each other's pockets because of the hours we spent each day, from 8.45 a.m. until 7 p.m. and by the time you got home and slept, it all started again. We were there as a family. The camaraderie we had was forged from a young age. I knew Michael Thomas from the age of 11. He was an outstanding footballer for his age compared to the rest of us, he had everything. I remember Tony Adams when he was a 12-year-old – he looked like a mod, with the old short jacket and short tonic trousers on. On the pitch he was exactly the same Tony Adams as he is the Arsenal and England captain. Even more than his play his authority stood out. You could always hear his voice, he was always organising everyone. We fought for each other like blood brothers.'

When Pat Rice became youth coach in the mid-'80s he hauled his youngsters into a meeting at Highbury to give them a rollicking: 'I read the riot act to them. "I'm asking you a straight question. How many of you lot are going to make it into the Arsenal first team?" David Rocastle went "*I will.*" He was the only one. "*I'll make it into the Arsenal first team. I'll do it.*" He had that desire and that fire in his belly.' David Dein recalls watching him for the South-East Counties side and rushing home, bursting to tell his family that he'd just seen a kid who could be a worldbeater. Arsenal expected.

This boy with the physique of a middleweight boxer, the energy of a sprinter and ball skills which might have been honed on the Copacobana, broke through aged 18. Rocky quivered with anticipation. 'The press came round and I had my big afro and white trousers and a white jumper and they said I looked like Tubbs out of *Miami Vice* – I got some stick from the lads about that. Unbelievable, though, my picture on the back page of the paper saying. "Young South London boy set to make his début for Arsenal tomorrow." It was a dreary 0–0 draw against Newcastle but to me it was the greatest game ever, I didn't want it to end. I realised I'd made my début for Arsenal.

'Whatever happens in life from now on, no one will ever be able to take away what I achieved. People always say you can't live in the past. Rubbish. You can't live in the past while you're still playing, but after you've finished there's no way anyone can take away the fact that I played that night at Anfield in 1989. That team will always live in Arsenal's minds. It will never be repeated – if it is then I'll be damned. With Michael and me in the side it was a dream come true for us, two kids coming through from the same area to make it into such a great Arsenal team. It was a fairy story, the man's version of Cinderella, especially when Michael scored the goal.

'I heard a lot of rumours that the reason Arsenal signed me in the first place was to get Michael, who was being chased by every single club imaginable, including Tottenham, Chelsea and Man United. I was good mates with Michael – you know how it is when you're younger – and we went on to the apprenticeship together.' The pair were spotted playing for South London Boys. It speaks volumes for David's sheer talent that he was picked for his district even though he didn't play for his school. His class wasn't allowed to have a team because the year above him had been banned. For fighting on the pitch.

If Rocastle thought he played a significant part in Thomas choosing Arsenal, he knew he was a prime mover in another South London brother from his childhood signing up at Highbury. 'He was a major reason for me joining,' says Ian Wright. 'He sold the club to me, he told me how the lads were.' The spirit, which got under Rocky's skin as a teenager, which drove George Graham's Arsenal to triumph. Wrighty liked the sound of that.

I Love the Lads

IAN WRIGHT

Arsenal 5 Southampton 1
2 May 1992

Seaman, Dixon, Winterburn, Hillier, Bould, Adams, Rocastle,
Wright, Campbell, Merson (Parlour), Limpar (Smith)

David Dein picks up the phone to Crystal Palace chairman Ron
Noades. 'Hello, Ron, will you release Mark Bright?'

'No,' rebuffs Noades.

'What about Ian Wright?'

'No.'

'Just give me a price.'

'It would have to be ridiculous. I genuinely don't want to sell
either of them, but if you offer me enough money I may have to.'

'Just give me a figure.'

'£2.5 million each.'

'Ron, that's a damn lot of money.'

'Well, if you offer it, I'll take it.'

'Ron, I'm offering you £2.5 million for Ian Wright.' There is
a deathly silence. 'Ron, I know you're a man of your word . . .'

'David, you've offered me £2.5 million. He's yours.'

★

George Graham must have had a funny turn. There is no alternative explanation. Why else, with the team scoring goals as if
their lives depended on it, would he break the club's transfer
record on a new striker? The Gunners had just notched 15 goals

133

in three games, which in itself stretches rationality to the limit, so he went out and bought Ian Wright. Naturally. One too many Boring Arsenal slurs must have penetrated his psyche. It certainly was an unexpected move, but it stands as the sale of the century. Much obliged, Ron.

However easy it was for Arsenal to negotiate with Noades, it was even easier to strike a deal with Ian. He strutted into Ken Friar's office and gabbled, 'Where do I sign?' Friar, ever the cautious, careful administrator, had never seen anyone so eager to put pen to paper. 'Hold on, Ian,' he said, 'Let's go through the contract and explain it all.' Ian didn't want to know. 'Just show me where to sign,' he babbled. Always impetuous, always making up for lost time, always wanting to do everything yesterday, he simply couldn't wait one more second to become an Arsenal player. And as soon as he was an Arsenal player he couldn't wait to get in the team. And as soon as he was in the team he couldn't wait to score a goal. The inner child in Wright is very much alive and kicking.

A few days short of his 28th birthday, this latecomer to the professional game grasped his elevation onto the big-time stage with a zeal that bordered on hyperactive. He is impossibly effervescent, outrageously energised. When he walks into a room he is the focus and when he leaves there is a void. Not to mention a sudden reduction in decibels. From the day he arrived Highbury was an altogether noisier place. George was well aware of the qualities he would bring to the squad: as a man he exudes wildness of character and fire in his soul and as a footballer he possesses explosive pace, a clinical eye for goal and a keen sense for the unpredictable. What the manager perhaps didn't realise was the extent to which all these traits would flourish at Highbury. Arsenal had never seen anything remotely like him in a red-and-white shirt. Instant hero.

During that pre-Wright 15-goal purple patch one of the teams swatted aside was Crystal Palace. '*Man, what a good team,*' thought Wright, as the goals rattled past. '*These forwards are unbelievable.*' Now he was on board, and raring to join in the fun. Smith picked up an injury so he marched straight into the team and marked his first Arsenal appearance in the Rumbelows Cup at Leicester with a goal. His smile outshone the floodlights.

It was merely an aperitif to an extraordinary starter served up on his league début three days later at Southampton. Smith returned and Davis dropped out so Ian was given the number 8 shirt, which he took to be a lucky charm, the number he wore on his first-ever football kit. With latent talent like his he didn't need luck, but he did feel he had something to prove. 'There was Alan Smith who had won the Golden Boot and Kevin Campbell who was someone they had a lot of faith in and pinned a lot of hopes on. The only way I could see myself staying in the side was by scoring goals.' No problem. Ian blitzed a scorching hat-trick. 'Even now when I see it on video I still get a funny kind of a tingly feeling,' he shakes his head in amazement. 'I felt like I was in amongst the real cream, people like Tony Adams, Dave Seaman, Lee Dixon, Nigel Winterburn, Michael Thomas, David Rocastle, Alan Smith, Merse, Anders, all of them Champions and internationals. I was really buzzing. Every move I made they found me with the ball. Every move! I noticed the difference in playing with guys like that immediately.

'After the Southampton game I felt I like I belonged amongst them. When you do something like that people accept you straight away. The boys were going, "*Jesus, that was unbelievable.*" George Graham told me it was the best début an Arsenal player has ever made. I remember him saying it in the lobby and I said "Cheers, boss, thanks very much," and walked straight off. I didn't appreciate it at the time, it didn't sink in because it was an unbelievable day.'

Rocastle, who scored the other goal at the Dell, was chuffed by the impact his old friend made. Ian had been staying at his house for a couple of days so they could travel to London Colney together enabling David to show him the ropes, and they were over-excited Arsenal room-mates, until the habit for chatting until five in the morning meant they had to be split up. When they got on the pitch, the wavelength they shared as children was still intact. 'It was perfect,' reminisces Rocky, 'exactly how we worked it when we played on the estate in Brockley. When he scored his hat-trick, we looked at each other wide-eyed, from playing in the park with each other to the Premiership with Arsenal. Incredible. He's five years older than me and I remember going round with my little mates to watch Ian and his mates playing football. Because they all thought they were Diego Maradonas nobody wanted to go in goal and someone would shout: *Oi, you, get in goal.* All these big giants whacked shots at us in between goals made of piles of coats. Ian was always outstanding, he would get the ball and do whatever he wanted with it.' No change there, then.

Like all great goalscorers, seeing the ball hit the back of the net is a constant compulsion for Wright, and like the best of his contemporaries – Gary Lineker, Alan Shearer, Robbie Fowler – his single-mindedness is overpowering. But what separates Ian from the others is the way he goes about it, with passion so raw it radiates from every pore. More than wearing his heart on his sleeve, his emotion is tattooed on his forehead, visible in his eyes, manifest in his charismatic celebrations. Every goal, to him, tastes of ambrosia and he crowns each mouthful with a vault into utopia. Whether it's a preening pose, a demented dance, a dramatic flop to the ground or a manic sprint into oblivion, the joy of the goal is milked to the full.

It's not very *Arsenal,* is it? This is supposed to be the dour, dull, dignified club. Outsiders may have sneered at the irony of a lunatic let loose in the Marble Halls, but for the faithful, Wrighty's regular outpourings of emotion bewitched us all. Anyway, the apparent contrast is deceptive: these two opposites attract because they are ideal to fill each other's needs. Arsenal of course benefit from Ian's sheer skill and exuberance, and the club provides him with a stable environment, a protective arm when he slips into trouble, which he does with reckless inevitability. It is all part of the 110 per cent man-on-a-mission package. It is the paradox of Ian Wright. Burning desire and breathless instinct both makes his game and renders him a split-second from losing it. When it comes to hitting the headlines he's in a class of his own, and with a mouth which moves with the same rapid, reflex action as his feet, you never know which part of his body will kickstart a story. Neither does he. Thus the victimised, misunderstood ego starts to brood when he courts criticism, and when he feels the whole world, or some muppet of a referee, is against him (which in his head often amounts to the same thing), the club is always ready to say *there, there.*

'With respect to things that happen off the field, the club's great,' says Ian. 'They really stick by players and that's the loyalty you need. That's why people like Tony Adams love the club, that's why I do. They stick by you when you need them. Whether or not it's psychology so that you will do your best for them, it works. When I get in trouble on the pitch I'm so psyched and wound up and pumped up because I want to do well, it overflows. But it's nothing other than just wanting to do good for the club. I'm proud of the club. George instilled that, he wanted you to be proud of the fact that you were at the Arsenal because he loved the club. When he used to have a go at someone he'd say how you didn't deserve to be wearing this shirt. That's why I try to play in a way that people can say I didn't leave any in the tank. I tried my best.'

One of his catchphrases is he'll *give it till it hurts,* and he recalls one game in particular which left him battered and shattered like no other. Three weeks after George Graham was sacked, with Arsenal sore and shaken and freefalling towards a relegation battle, the team travelled to Auxerre in the Cup-Winners' Cup for what was one of the most vital matches in modern times. There was a palpable sense that defeat would send Arsenal careering into further decline and, heaven forbid, tumbling out of the Premiership. The Gunners were in urgent need of a booster, and against a meticulously organised French side who were unlucky to draw 1–1 in the first leg at Highbury, the prospects were grim. It was win or bust.

The entire team gave it till it hurt. 'It was so hard, it was so relentless. David Seaman had three broken ribs and when you're watching him having six injections before the game, those are the kind of things that build the spirit up,' Ian declares. 'We ran and ran, worked and worked, and it really did hurt afterwards, you know. Physically, in the dressing-room, it *hurt.* It was really painful, all the kicks we took. But it was worth it because we won.' Wright struck a goal of trademark opportunism, an unexpected chip from way out which sailed over the keeper's head. He sank to his knees and raised his eyes to the skies, believing he had been blessed by a touch of divine inspiration.

Reacting to a goal is an expression of spontaneous emotion, and depending on the circumstances, a goal can elicit pure joy, or reviving relief, or maddened defiance, or simple admiration, and, on those rarest of occasions, virtual insanity. The Arsenal fans in the Stade de l'Abbé Deschamps were overwhelmed by a mélange of all these feelings, such was the overriding importance of the game. As usual, Ian Wright delivered when we needed it most. The Gunners were under attack for the other 89 minutes of the game, the team defended like a pride of lions, and it finished Auxerre 0 Arsenal 1. The path to salvation was paved.

Funny how there was a fad at Highbury for number 8 shirts adorned by the word 'God'. As a religious man, Wrighty's rather humbled by it – although as a narcissist perhaps he secretly enjoys it. 'If they put "Second to God",' he muses, 'I'd be really pleased.'

While his Arsenal career was in its infancy, after such a dynamic start, it seemed nothing could go wrong. Going well in the league, buoyant after a brilliant performance at Lisbon's Stadium of Light in the European Cup, the team visited Highfield Road in the Rumbelows Cup. Coventry 1 Arsenal 0. Oh, well. It's a tinpot trophy anyway. With Benfica coming to Highbury in a week's time the Gunners had their eye on more valuable silverware. Ian was cup-tied for the match against the Portuguese champions, but he knew he would be eligible for the next round, and, having got that crucial away goal in a creditable draw in the first leg, Arsenal were odds-on favourites to progress. Arsenal 1 Benfica 3. 'It was a nightmare,' Wrighty groans. 'I came to Arsenal because I wanted to play European football and to be so close, one game away from the European Cup, we lost. We made so many chances that night and the vein I was in at the time I knew that if I had played I would have scored. It was so frustrating.'

It got worse before it got better. On the subject of nightmares, an FA Cup third-round tie at Wrexham was a cold-sweated, fall-out-of-bed-with-a-bump horror. Like Benfica, Ian watched from the stands. At half-time he chuckled with the lads as untroubled Arsenal led 1–0. 'I thought *We're gonna romp this*. Me and Merse were in the toilet, messing about keeping the ball up, and Merse was smiling, "What's the score going to be?" It was like the kiss of death. We were laughing, *Just imagine if they beat us!* . . . They beat us. It was like someone throwing freezing cold water all over you. *Whoosh*.'

Apart from the fact it left the giant floored and sobbing with sorry shame, it also brought the rude awakening every club dreads in the New Year. Arsenal were out of every competition by January. Having been unceremoniously turfed out of three Cups and taken a dip in the league which took the Championship beyond reach, morale shrivelled. 'It was a downer,' reflects Ian, 'What are we playing for?' Good question. Bearing in mind the answer is not a lot, what occurred during the remainder of the season was startling. Arsenal launched into an unbeaten run from February to May which produced the most breathtakingly beautiful football Highbury has possibly ever seen. Sheffield Wednesday were pummelled 7–1; Crystal Palace were slaughtered 4–1; Liverpool were annihilated 4–0; Southampton were trounced 5–1. Just about every goal was a pearl.

Arsenal's forward line – Limpar, Wright, Smith, Campbell, Merson – became a fearsome five who slammed goals past anyone who came their way. Ian reckons it was as good as it gets in terms of attacking football. 'We were good professionals all playing together at a peaky kind of time. Everything I was doing was coming off and I was scoring left, right and centre, Anders was brilliant, Merse was brilliant, Alan was brilliant, Kevin was the one who started it off against Sheffield Wednesday. It was 1–1 for a long time and he came off the bench and scored this fantastic goal on the turn, and that was enough to spark the rest of us off [he clicks his fingers] just like that.

'I think there's a chemistry when you're enjoying yourselves and we were all buzzing so much we couldn't wait to get out there. It was just *happening*, people were moving and hitting great shots and goals were flying in everywhere. I don't know what it was that made us gel. The others had worked together for a while, and when I came in it could have messed things up a little bit, but I just tried to go with the flow. There was something in everybody to contribute to the five of us doing well – Kevin was strong, Merse was artistic, Anders was unpredictable, Alan was holding up, and I was there to sniff it out and score. Everyone had a job and when all five of us were playing it really did happen. It really did.'

With everyone in such hypnotic form, the opposition were totally bamboozled. Try to stop Wright from poaching and he would create for his team-mates; try to stop Merson from striking and he would feed an onrushing colleague; try to stop Campbell from shooting, the others would pounce; throw Limpar into the equation and defenders were on their knees begging the referee to put them out of their misery. During that game against Wednesday Ian played the role of provider rather than finisher but he still managed to get on the score-sheet, and it was the start of a devastating run of 13 goals in 14 games which enlivened an intriguing head to head with Gary Lineker for the Golden Boot.

Wrighty is full of gratitude to the lads who helped him lead this fiesta. 'Alan Smith was fantastic for me. He took a lot of knocks, sometimes when I was wheeling away when I scored Alan was picking himself up off the floor where he'd just been clattered to get the ball through to me. Those are the kind of things, you see it happening so many times, which make you think *God, look how much work he's doing for me to score.* That's when you appreciate world-class players, the players around you.

'Anders is the type of player I'd give anything to have in the side because he wants his striker to score. He'd come up to me before the game and say, "Come on, Gary Lineker's only two goals behind you, you need to score more." I scored four against Everton but I always say that was the Anders show – he made every goal for me. When he laid on my hat-trick, he could have just lifted it over Neville Southall himself but he squared it to me. Those things I never forget. That season he set up a good 90 per cent of my goals. I got on well with him; sometimes he was his own little guy in his own little world, but when we were playing he got very pumped up in his own little way. I was pleased that I played with him for the time I did and I owe a lot of the start of my Arsenal career to Anders. I dedicate my first Arsenal year to him – he really did do well for me.'

Ian's first season exceeded all his wildest expectations and, with an imagination as unrestrained as his, that's going some. 'When I played against Liverpool the season before, Palace were beaten 9–0 and here I was with Arsenal beating them 4–0. Even Sheffield Wednesday, it was a tough game for Palace, a really massive game, and here we were beating them 7–1. I just couldn't believe the change. Emotionally, it was unbelievable; I was on cloud nine for the whole of the time since I signed until the season ended.' He was close to cloud ten at White Hart Lane in his first North London derby on enemy territory. Losing 1–0 with a minute to go, the Tottenham fans indulging in merciless Gunner-baiting, informing Arsenal's £2.5 million man he was a waste of money, Wrighty slid the ball home. The saviour struck again and he was in paradise. 'It really did knock 'em back,' he smiles. 'When you score it and the ground goes [he takes a sharp intake of breath] and then you hear our fans go mad and you can see their fans hands on heads, you realise that you've just virtually ripped their hearts out their bodies, you know? The derby is a game I just love.' That's why Arsenal adore him; that's why others abhor him. Whenever Ian Wright is on the pitch it's a white-knuckle ride.

2 May. Southampton at home. This is it. A day we all knew was coming. A day which Arsenal Football Club would never forget. A day which marked the passing of the North Bank. For 79 years supporters stood on that grand concrete terrace and now was the time to say goodbye to a friend so many of us called home. The bulldozers were due on Monday morning. A powerful sense of history hung heavy in the Highbury air.

Maybe it was appropriate that the North Bank's newest hero should send the old place off in sensational style. As one emblem of Arsenal departs, so a fresh one takes a major step into the club's story. The man with an eye on the Golden Boot is at the beginning of a spell which will in all probability end with him holding the honour of the club's greatest-ever goalscorer. Wright never suffers under the pressure expectation brings. 'I thrive on it,' he says. 'Once you get out there, just do it. Pressure is something you feel before or after games but while you're playing you just do the do. Just shoot.'

Ian is one goal behind Lineker, who is playing at Old Trafford in his last game for Tottenham before leaving for Japan. The friendly rivalry between the two strikers gives the contest added edge – North London telephone banter had been exchanged after every goal in the run-in. Early in the game Wright scores, but his effort is disallowed for a dubious offside. Quite out of character, he doesn't dash to remonstrate with the referee. Why not? 'Dunno,' he mumbles. 'I couldn't believe it, though.' At half-time it's 0–0 at Highbury and Lineker has scored in Manchester. Wrighty now needs a hat-trick and another dose of divine intervention to stop Saint Gary striking again.

Into the second half, and we're shooting towards the North Bank. Ian steps onto the pitch and into a bullet train heading for goal. Benali, who is always worth at least one goal to any team playing against Southampton, fouls Merson in the area. '*Penalty!*' hollers the North Bank. Dixon, the regular spot-kick man, nods at Wrighty. Were you nervous, Ian? 'No,' he says. As if. 'Mind you, Merse said, "Come on, you better score," and then I felt scared. If the boys don't say anything I'm all right. But then I just did my routine and scored. I practise them and I'm so confident in myself, I don't care how important the game is. If a goalkeeper can save my penalty when I do my routine right, he's good. Very good.' One down, two to go.

Last minute of the season, a phrase which has a familiar ring to it, and Seaman throws the ball out to Ian, deep in his own half. 'I got it and thought, *Right, I'm just gonna go for it now.*' Displaying the tunnel vision of Linford Christie, he blocked out the rest of the world and ran. Hurlock, a monster who could probably knock over Giant Haystacks if he was in the mood, closes in on Ian. But nothing will distract the lynx-eyed livewire from his goal mission. He whizzes past him and wallops the ball into the back of the net. Two down, one to go. Rocastle grabs Wrighty and says, 'You really have to have it, boy.' From kick-off Arsenal charge towards the North Bank and the ball breaks to Ian. 'I tried to slot it in past him and it hit me high up on the shin and went in. That's when I thought it's my destiny to win it.

'I was so pleased and proud that I scored a hat-trick in front of the North Bank before they knocked it down, to see off that great legend of terraces. To think how long it had been there, that people have been watching football there for years. Grandads who have watched there from when they were kids. It was such a fitting tribute. 2 May, I'll never forget it. I cried because it was emotional. At the end I found out Gary Lineker was one behind me and I was top scorer. To beat Gary Lineker as well! He phoned me up later in the night to congratulate me. I've got a lot of respect for him. It would have been nice if we'd won the Championship and I won the Golden Boot but it doesn't work like that. I think I'd have been too greedy going to a club like Arsenal and expecting to do all that in one season. It can't go that good, you know.'

Boring, boring Arsenal scored 92 goals and George Graham was entitled to feel smug. But for all the pleasure of the rampant attack, a niggle festered at the back of his mind: the club finished trophyless. He tinkered with his master plan. More emphasis would be thrust on Ian Wright than ever before. Midfield artists would give way to artisans who would work and work to give the ball to the goalaholic. 'When Anders and Merse were on song they were breathtaking, but like all good things it couldn't go on forever,' George reflects. 'I realised when they weren't on song they were both off song at the same time. You can only afford to carry one winger in English football – if he comes in for little spasms that's fine, but when Merse and Anders had an off day we were playing with nine men. I thought, *I've got to go with one* and I selected Merse.' It seemed inexplicable, but Limpar was shunned, Rocastle was sold, and without their subtle promptings from midfield the freescoring glee disappeared from Arsenal as suddenly as it arrived. Ian excepted. You could hit him with a sledgehammer and he'd crave goals while he was unconscious.

In Limpar, George discovered that the most alluring things in life can be the most bewildering. It had dawned on him as early as the Championship season of 1991. 'By the end of November he had scored eight goals and I said to him, "Anders, the way you're going here you're going to finish up with 20-odd goals."

He turned round and I couldn't believe when he said, "Mr Graham, I won't." I said, "Why? What do you mean?" He says, "I'm not a goalscorer."' George shakes his head disbelievingly. 'Right there and then I realised he had no confidence in himself. He honestly believed that he wasn't a goalscorer, he was a negative thinker right from the off. I kept saying, "You can, Anders, you can! You can score!"' The Super Swede, whose dazzling invention illuminated Arsenal's title trail, only struck three more league goals that season, all of them on the last day of the season almost six months later. George worried about his attitude.

So, Limpar, sultry stunning sublime Limpar, got the treatment Graham reserved for players who tried his patience; randomly juggled between the team, the bench and the reserves, and finally released. Frustrating times, as the team was infinitely poorer without him. George shrugs. 'Anders was just pure raw magnificent talent. But the lads used to say when we were playing away from home, they would know in the first five minutes if Anders was on song or if they were playing with ten men. Sadly, a wasted talent.'

What about Rocky? One thing *he* never lacked was belief. 'The main reason I sold David Rocastle was because the medical advice I got was that he had an arthritic knee and it would be a problem,' states George. 'Quite a few footballers play with it, but the problem is you can play matches but have to be very careful about training. The trouble with David was that as soon as he stopped training he ballooned. This was always in the papers, and this is the problem with being a manager: You can't tell the truth because you're devaluing or criticising one of your own players. I couldn't tell people that we couldn't train him too hard.'

Rocastle disagrees: 'George says my knee might have restricted me but I think that's a cop-out. If he checks his training records I never missed a day. I could understand if my knee was like Gazza's but I've had one operation and two clean-outs – it's like brushing your teeth, you're back playing in ten days. I did put weight on – to be honest I let myself go for a little while which might have been more down to depression than the fact I wasn't training as hard as I could. If George sold me when my knee was allegedly in bad shape, how come I passed a five-hour medical with Leeds and was their record signing? I've had three moves in my time and surely a doctor will tell. But the rumours persist and sometimes I feel like banging my head against a wall. I might have a problem with my knee when I'm 50 and I've finished playing but I'm prepared to make that sacrifice. I couldn't believe I was being sold by Arsenal at the time. Everybody thinks that they'll probably stay at the club forever and I thought I had a good few years left in me. It didn't happen. It was one of my saddest days, because it was my home. In the end you've got to try and live with it.'

Two conflicting stories, then. George thinks David's knee wasn't up to the task and David thinks it was. Look at Paul McGrath, a man with the same condition who is one of the finest defenders in football at the age of 37. Living proof that even if you can't train hard you can play hard. And David still believes he can do both. Ultimately, the manager took a calculated gamble. He had a team to run, and didn't want to bank on a player he wasn't sure he could push to the limits, and he had a business to run, and at the time of sale Rocky commanded a £2 million fee. Nobody ever said football was fair.

Ian was bitterly disappointed to see both his best pal and his favourite assists man depart. 'When Rocky left I was gutted,' he admits. 'I was crying and Tony told the boss, "You better have a word," because I didn't look like I was dealing with it well, and I wasn't. As for Anders, he could play to such a standard, and to reach that standard consistently is very hard. That's what makes great players – because they can. George Graham said to me, to everyone, that he wants performing stars, he doesn't want show-pieces, he wants people doing it all the time. He demanded it, and because Anders didn't deliver it because he's got a different mentality to English players, they fell out and frustrations got worse and worse between the pair of them. When he left it was a sad, sad day for us.

'George respects people who realise how lucky they are to be footballers and know that they mustn't take it for granted, and always have the desire to play the best they can every time they go out there. Maybe that is why he and Anders didn't get on because Anders couldn't always do that, but he maybe saw in me that no matter how bad it was going for me I would still give everything I've got.'

★

The predator continued to stalk goals, play the showman, slip involuntarily into indiscipline. The usual. Just another life in the day of Ian Wright. And then he lost his spark. The joker was morose. His glinting smile turned into a smouldering frown. Instead of waking up every day feeling glad to be alive, he was gloomy. It was the consequence of a sticky personality clash. When Bruce Rioch became manager of Arsenal Ian felt oppressed by football for the first time in his life. His appetite dwindled and, without it, he became sullen and subversive, his energy rerouted from positive to negative. Incapable of playing his feelings with a discreet, delicate hand, Wrighty huffed. And when he huffs everyone knows about it.

He didn't want to play for Rioch. 'That's what I wrote in my transfer request,' he asserts. 'I don't want to play for you no more. I'm playing for the boys, I'm not playing for you. I didn't like his aggressive approach, that's why we didn't get on. He had a problem with me because I think he expected me to have a chip on my shoulder and a blasé attitude but I trained well, and I played how I trained. He was always looking for excuses to try and have a go at me. I had a go at him back and I feel I was justified in doing that. A club as great as ours shouldn't have a manager like that. We should have a manager like Arsène Wenger, forward-thinking, creative people, not old school bullies who shout in your ear like a sergeant-major. You can't frighten people and get the best out of them. Under Bruce Rioch I fell out of love with football; and it wasn't the game, it was one man's view. It was the first time since I was eight years old that I felt like I didn't want to play.

'I'm just pleased the club was strong enough and had the foresight to say, "It ain't working, we've got to move on," because otherwise people like Steve Hughes wouldn't be coming through now. I used to speak to Steve and at one stage Rioch had got him so down he didn't even want to play football any more. That is sad. He's a manager, not a person who should discourage you from playing the greatest game in the world. I'm really pleased for Steve now, he'll be a regular. And when he does and he's not playing well, I'll say to him, *Remember the times when you weren't playing how desperate you were to play? Think back to those times.* It's all good stuff, you know? I am relieved I didn't leave because I wouldn't want to be missing out on these great times that we are going into, which will happen just at the twilight of my career. I can ease out with Arsenal right bang on top, like when I came here.' Under Wenger, Ian feels like he's on a second honeymoon with the club. He said it best when he hoisted his shirt over his head to reveal the message *I love the lads.* He can't get enough of that Arsenal thang.

The Frenchman is amazed by him. 'Take any manager in the world, give him Ian Wright and he will be surprised,' he smiles. 'He is just surprising, every day something new.' If the Brazilians play to the beat of the samba, Ian plays to the spirit of jazz – full of natural improvisation, unconventional rhythms and melodies flowing freely from the heart – fused with a blast of groovy funk. John Coltrane meets James Brown. The music in his soul keeps Ian buzzing, hungry for football, striving for success, yearning for the thrill of scoring. He's a goal junkie. At the end of Wenger's first season he has the Arsenal all-time goalscoring record in his sights. When he reached his century David Dein alerted him to the possibility of topping the charts, giving the poacher a piece of paper which read *Cliff Bastin 178 goals in 396 games, John Radford 149 goals in 481 games, Ian Wright 100 goals in 139 games.* Ian pointed to Bastin's name. 'That's my aim,' he said. 'That's my aim.'

Like George Graham, Wrighty is one of those people who joined the club from outside only to become as obsessed, possibly more obsessed, than those who grow up there. The colourful, wild boy whose personality seemed to be at odds with steady, traditional Highbury feels a closeness to the club which over-whelms him. 'It has completely taken over my life,' he confesses. 'I think now, for the rest of my life, everything will be Arsenal. I feel like I'm an Arsenal person just like Tony Adams is. I absolutely love the club. Because I was born in Woolwich where Arsenal originated, they say I was destined to play for Arsenal.' He speaks with the infectious enthusiasm of a dyed-in-the-wool supporter. And he behaves like one, too. Ian is a regular in the stands at Highbury to watch the reserves, and on one famous occasion, during another of his rather too numerous suspensions, he went to watch the first team at Crystal Palace from the un-ethical vantage-point of a seat in the middle of all the Gooners. 'I wasn't going to go because the Palace fans always give me so much stick,' he recalls, 'So I went with the Arsenal fans, protec-ted by my people. It was brilliant.' Only Wrighty would dream of doing that. Imagine, say, Cantona mixing it with the crowd at Selhurst Park. Mmm, maybe not.

Evergreen though he is, and not many 33-year-olds score 30 goals a season, he knows the day will eventually come when he has to hang up those golden boots, and he hopes to stay at High-bury to groom future strikers. '*Anelka, man . . .*' he rhapsodises. Not for Ian a step down a division to earn a wage. 'I'm not cut out for that because I'm a volatile guy by nature. When I get older I will still be trying to close in on people and I'll be slower and kicking people and getting booked and sent off and people will remember me for those things. I don't want that. Imagine me coming back in the Cup with some team and Arsenal win 6–0, which would be great for the club, but people will be saying *Look at Ian Wright in that team* and *Why don't they put that old dog to sleep?* I wouldn't want that. I'll stop playing here and go to do something with the youth team which will be good because I'll be Arsenal for the rest of my life.'

In one respect he'll always be in London N5. If you follow the road round from Arsenal tube, 200 yards up Drayton Park there is a new block of flats called 'Ian Wright House'. He went to open the building, and sometimes drives past just to see his name above the entrance. He once took his mum to see it and she burst into tears. 'I can't believe that my name is on somebody's letters every day!' he exclaims. 'Really strange. I'm very proud. I owe it to the people around Highbury to break the record. They want me up there.' The motivation still burns as strongly as ever. The ambition still glows as tantalisingly as ever. For Wrighty, the buzz never stops. 'When you get an opportunity, you have to do the most you can, or else it's pointless taking that opportunity in the first place. If you're not going to reach for the stars, you know, you may as well do something else.'

Overcome

TONY ADAMS

Arsenal 2 Sheffield Wednesday 1 (aet)
20 May 1993

Seaman, Dixon, Winterburn, Davis, Linighan, Adams, Jensen,
Wright (O'Leary), Smith, Merson, Campbell

Captain Fantastic. Captain Courageous. Captain Colossus. Since
the day he became the club's youngest-ever skipper aged 21, Tony
Adams has been Arsenal's tower of strength. From the highs of
silver-lined triumph to the lows of dark losses, Tony stood up to
be counted. Unfailingly. Picture him inspiring his men to beat
the odds in Copenhagen during the 1994 Cup-Winners' Cup
Final, hands pounding together, face contorted, larynx strained
as he booms encouragement. Or imagine him in Paris a year
later, stoically grabbing the agony of failure and forcing it to
release its vice-like grip. While his team-mates lie prostrate on the
turf he goes to lift them with a reassuring hand and a comforting
utterance. Then in the dressing-room he gives a rousing speech
to raise his crestfallen colleagues: *Remember this, remember and it
will push us to more trophies.* When he's finished they respond with
an emotional ovation. It's stirring stuff, but then that's always
been the way with Tony.

'We've had a lot of good times here but you don't know how
good they are until you have the bad ones,' Adams claims. Then
he lowers his voice, hushed to barely a whisper, and stares, as if
he's eyeballing defeat from an inch away. 'I always appreciated
the Luton Towns when we lost in '88, the semi-final against Tot-

tenham in '91, real painful horrible losses. You get so much from it, you really do. If you can try to capture that it will motivate you so much more for next time. The feeling, to not to let that happen to you again, is amazing. The semi-final, Luton and Zaragoza, I learned more from them than lifting any trophy. I learned more from all my defeats than anything I learned from my successes.'

Likewise in life. He has gleaned more, grown more, from his personal traumas. Qualities like bravery and guts, which are so regularly attributed to Tony on the field, were never more evident than when he gathered his team-mates together at London Colney to confess he was an alcoholic. The tower might have looked superficially stable but internally it was crumbling, and Tony recognised the only person who could instigate the repairs was himself. *That* takes bravery and guts. This leader of men decided to help Tony Adams, to lead the man whose problems were so far down the list he had never got that far.

This crux came at a time when the club was in a state of turmoil – managers were coming and going as if they were aboard a conveyor belt running through North London, and after the Zaragoza game the team of winners didn't look like winning any more. Tony, more than anyone, bore the weight of responsibility for Arsenal Football Club on his shoulders. Tony's a colossus, we thought. Tony would keep it all together. Tony could cope with anything. That's a hell of an onus to lay on one man. Way too much, evidently. We built him up as the Atlas who could carry Arsenal's world, and nobody stopped for a moment even to conceive the possibility he might be vulnerable. He was so damn good at analysing and reacting to the team's needs that nobody gave a second's thought to the fact he might be neglecting his own. He was disillusioned and he wanted out. 'I don't want to stick around a team of also-rans. I don't want to be battling every week at the bottom of the table, I want to win things. I can't deny that was in me,' he says. 'But because I had a load of other problems the football kind of shifted as a priority, which maybe stopped me from being a man, because if I was a man I might have gone.'

Football was his anchor, the one aspect of his life which he was absolutely assured about, and yet it also weighed him down to such a degree he was sinking with it. 'To a certain extent football took over my life because you go from game to game and you forget the bit in between,' he explains. 'I feel like I've not had a Monday, Tuesday, Thursday or Friday in my life. I feel like I just live Wednesday and Saturday, which is a pretty unbelievable scenario, but you do when you've got your head concentrated in the football world. You go *bang, bang, bang* from game to game . . . and 18 years later you're here reflecting on it all. Me? I always put me to the back. Oh, I'm not important. Now I've changed. I've kind of chilled out a bit, as Ian might say. I thought I was the dog's bollocks and now I realise there are things I can learn from other people. I'm better at balancing it now, I can help out individuals and I can also get my own bits and pieces in order. I'm starting to live, and it's only come through experience, that I kind of have a Monday and a Tuesday, I try to have my other days. Learn from your mistakes but get on with your life.'

He did exactly that. And it took considerable courage and immense iron will to do so. He used those features which are hallmarks of his game to reinvent himself as a person. Now, he tries to detach himself from the stereotype of Tony Adams the colossus. He takes the mickey out of his old machismo. He cringes at words like *pride* and *leader* and emits an air of embarrassed cynicism towards his popular image. If he could remove himself from the public eye's incessant, intrusive stare, he would. If he can deflect praise, he does. He just wants to be a self-effacing, low-key fellow who plays football to the best of his ability, enjoys his life, and does his best. 'You get on with your job at the end of the day. You come in and try to get back to basics. I keep things simple. What can I do? I can play football. So I get on with that, and a lot of people around me get on with it too. Because we are all good footballers we do okay.

'I always believed I was a bloody good footballer. I try to be a humble guy but I've got genuine belief in what I can do. I'm never going to be an Alan Shearer, I'm never going to be a Paul Gascoigne, I'm never going to be a Dave Seaman, but my particular job that I can do, I feel I can do it very well. I've never had a problem with confidence because I always believed, even from when I was a small kid, that I could do it.

'I used to come in and go, "All right, son?" to David O'Leary when I was 17 years old. He couldn't believe it. But I don't think you can get away with it unless you've got the backup of the talent, otherwise you can kiss goodbye to that arrogance and flashness. Because I was delivering the goods as well it was, *He's okay, this kid, he's helping us. Let's let him in.*'

It's hardly surprising young Tony had swagger. As a teenager playing in an exhibition match at the FA centre at Lilleshall a gaggle of coaches watched him in amazement, wondering who this kid was who looked like a new Bobby Moore in the making. At Arsenal he leapfrogged the youth team altogether and bounded straight into the reserves, then became the youngest-ever player to represent the first team, shortly after his 17th birthday. By the time he was 20 he had played for England. 'I had no fear of football at all,' he states. 'Football has always been such a great area for me. I've had injury problems and health problems and family problems and relationship problems, like all of us, but the one area of my life that has always been pretty successful, by the grace of God, has been my football. It's all gone into place.'

★

It was George Graham who first dubbed Tony Adams a colossus. It's the frustration of every manager that he can't cross that white line to influence events on the pitch, and in his captain, George had somebody out there who represented everything he required from his players during a game. Tony was Arsenal's bedrock. He led by example and every player was expected to do his utmost to imitate those standards.

Just as important was the impression Tony made on the team outside the 90 minutes of play. Take Ian Wright's arrival at the club. 'When he came I kind of put my arm round Ian in a nice way,' says Adams. 'The conflicting person that he is, he's always trying to look for ways out. If you say sit he'll stand, that's his character. I said to Wrighty, "Look, Ian, look at George. This is the way George and I and the team get success here. You can be a part of that if you want to be, it's okay. You can do it your way and you can have the conflict, and you're always going to score goals, but maybe just have a look at this . . ." It kind of worked. I needed to do that because he's a bugger. Some players have got it in them, and Ian's one of them, he'd die for himself and he'd die for this club because he wants success. It's not in all players but Ian has that ambition and drive in him: *I want to do well, I want to score goals.* All you've got to do is point him in the right direction. Simple as that.' Like all exceptional captains, Tony had his finger on the pulse of the team and he knew how to get the optimum response out of all the diverse characters. The manager was extremely fortunate to have him around.

'Son of George' was a nickname which did the rounds in the Arsenal dressing-room. It was handed through the team according to who the boss held up as his paragon of virtue. 'During the course of the season he would have favourites,' remembers Alan Smith. 'You'd be the blue-eyed boy one week. In team meetings he'd say, "Oh, Alan did well. Look at him, I want you to copy Alan." And you're sitting there squirming. Please don't, George. Then obviously in training afterwards everyone pulled your leg about it. Because George wasn't somebody you could get close to, if he did show a bit of favouritism the boys went, "Ooh, he loves you, doesn't he?"' But it was different with the captain. 'Tony was permanent Son of George,' smiles Smith. Graham was full of respect for Adams because they shared that addiction to winning, that capacity to stop at nothing in order to succeed.

Tony was resourceful, forever finding new ways to imbue a winning mentality in the team. He didn't just practise every trick in the book, he also unearthed a couple of unorthodox methods. He sought little nuggets of information to use as lucky charms, and if one didn't exist he'd make something up. 'It got to the stage where I was inventing things, being the compulsive liar I was at that stage of my life, for the boys' benefit to give them belief. I remember one just before Copenhagen. "The last time we won in Europe, we played West Ham last home game of the season. Great omen that." The belief was palpable, *Yeah, it's our turn again! We were gonna win it, you know.* The little ones I've come out with are amazing. Some of them were actually true.' His eyes glint. 'Belief. Whatever wins, don't knock it.'

Arsenal's 1993 Cup campaign started to gather momentum in

the New Year and Tony was on a roll. Within a week the Gunners faced trips to Yeovil in the FA Cup third round and Scarborough in the Coca-Cola Cup fourth round. Played in pea-soupers so thick the ball could barely be seen through the cotton wool atmosphere, and coming a year after Wrexham, the critics licked their lips in anticipation of another potential slaying. Tony had other ideas. 'That's another omen, Yeovil, going back to the Double. I fed that one in as well.' He grins broadly. 'We went down there and Wrighty smashed them with a hat-trick, then to Scarborough. Nigel Winterburn scores? David O'Leary plays midfield? You've got to win the Cup, it's as simple as that. Listen, you're going to win the Cup if you've got David in midfield and Nigel scoring a goal. I didn't even have to go out against these teams, we should have just picked up the Cup at the start of the first game. Amazing how it works, isn't it.'

Just as well Tony managed to inject a modicum of belief because league form was unbelievably poor. After the goal rush of the previous season, Arsenal failed to find the net in almost half their Premiership games. A plethora of dismal performances of unendurable drabness turned Highbury into penury as far as the Championship was concerned. 'The league was a grind,' admits Tony. *'Jesus, 0–0; 0–0 again; lost 0–1. Hard games, tough games, try and keep it together. Oh God, we've created nothing again today. We're not making any chances, we're not scoring . . .* I think we were stale. We were a different side with Ian in the team. He's a tremendous goalscorer and you need to feed him. We always knew if we keep things solid then this boy is going to score goals for us. That was a big emphasis on what we were going to do.

'That's what made us a great Cup side because we could keep it tight and we had someone who could score. You get in the Cup, you defend well, the other team gets frustrated: *boom* you've nicked it 1–0 and you're in the next round. But week in, week out, you can't rely on that to win Championships. You've got to go away from home and if you've only got one player who can score for you it becomes very difficult, and at home you've simply got to create. Even if you're defensively very good, if you can't create you're thinking *Jesus, we're at Highbury, we've got to go forward today.* It can get very difficult and I think it was reflected in some of the home performances. Our league football was dreadful, I think we were in a bit of schtuck. But Cup games, the one-off, we knew we had the potential to be very good.' Indeed. For schizophrenic Arsenal the knock-out competitions offered light-headed rushes of relief from the interminable migraine of the league programme.

Leeds are Arsenal's next opponents in the FA Cup, and after a 2–2 draw at home – not having witnessed four goals in a game at Highbury for six months it was the height of excitement – the boys traipsed to Elland Road. Good omen? Arsenal won in Yorkshire at the same stage of the same competition two years previously. It's a thriller. 'One of the best games I've ever played in during my career, really enjoyable,' nods Tony. One-nil up, two-one down, Wrighty comes off the bench like a boxer dog let off a leash after serving a suspension for belting Tottenham's David Howells, and equalises in the last minute. In extra-time he smacks a rasping shot so powerful the Leeds keeper gets his hands to it but it stings off his palms and into the net regardless: 3–2. 'Thank you, Mr John Lukic, he done us a lovely favour,' Tony lets out a big laugh.

Next up Nottingham Forest at home for the fifth round. Good omen? Arsenal had just beaten them 2–0 at Highbury in the fifth round of the League Cup thanks to a brace from that man Wright. The supreme striker must have believed all the portents as the game is a replica and he fires another pair. The dual-powered Cup run begins to gather speed. Crystal Palace are the opponents in the Coca-Cola semi-final – good omen? Last time Arsenal won the League Cup they beat a London club in the last four – and are duly brushed aside.

The FA Cup quarter-final draw takes Arsenal to Portman Road. Good omen? Alan Sunderland, who scored the winner last time we won the Cup, has a pub in Ipswich and is coming to the game. The sight of a handful of Gooners dressed up in curly wigs, false moustaches and 1979 shirts having a pint in Alan's pub brings a smile to the old boy's face. (Incidentally, references to Roger Osborne and the 1978 final are to be ignored. That doesn't have any relevance at all.) Arsenal win 4–2 and Tony nets his first goal of the season.

★

The sound of palpitating heartbeats throbs in houses all over North London and South Yorkshire. Supporters of Arsenal, Tottenham, Sheffield United and Sheffield Wednesday gawp at the television, too daunted to blink, as Graham Kelly and friends at Lancaster Gate rustle four balls around the velvet bag. It is either two derbies in the FA Cup semi-finals or a possible derby in the final. Ten seconds later and Tottenham fans are nostalgically reliving Gascoigne's free-kick while Arsenal fans are leaping round the front room yelling *REVENGE!* in a tone more bloody desperate than boldly defiant. It can't happen again. It can't.

There is absolutely no place for omens in the build-up to this one, with the 3–1 defeat in 1991 still horribly fresh in the mind. Gazza telephones all his old team-mates to send positive vibes from his new home in Italy, and to top it all, the time-honoured symbol of superstition that is the Chinese calendar calls 1993 the Year of the Cockerel. 'The pressure of the previous encounter unsettled some of the lads,' remarks Tony. 'We were quite apprehensive. When you've got so much pressure involved it's hard not to realise what it would have meant to lose. It could have happened.' The semi-final sequel is consumed by such acerbic tension that Wembley is a pacifist's hell. It's the kind of raw encounter where fear of defeat is paramount.

For Arsenal there are ghosts to be exorcised and the man with the power to do so is Tony Adams. Late in the second half Merson hovers over a free-kick as the six-footers arrive with intent in the box. 'I always remember walking up – I've had this conversation with the Tottenham lads since – for some reason they only had two people marking three of us and I noticed it,' Tony recalls. 'One of their big lads went into the wall because it was a free-kick, and he should have been marking at the far post. I saw Andy Linighan with Neil Ruddock and as we were walking forward into the box I said, "*Andy, take him inside.*" Ruddock has to do his job, he has to go with the first man, and it left me in acres of space just to head it in. It was wonderful. Great ball wasn't it, from Merse. We worked on it many times in training.'

He raises his eyebrows. 'The best-laid plans are the ones you don't work at.'

Tony heads the ball into the net and is engulfed. Linighan, Wright and Campbell are first to embrace him, their wild faces something to behold. Meanwhile at the other end of the pitch David Seaman collapses to his knees, arms outstretched, with a beam as wide as Wembley's plains. He of all people needed this result to unfetter the suffering of 1991, when his uncommon errors shot Arsenal in the foot. This time he foils Tottenham feet. Early in the game he had faced a one-on-one and stooped to conquer. 'He very much won the game the same as I had,' adds Tony.

The sheer relief of the goal stokes up Arsenal's belief and Tottenham never look capable of breaking it, even when the Gunners are reduced to ten men after Dixon is sent off for a second bookable offence. 'I felt really strong, because I've been in that situation many times before,' says Tony. 'I called upon a bit of my experience just to round up a few folks and keep driving.' Rarely has a final whistle sounded so divine for Arsenal, the signal for two years of gnawing hurt to evaporate. No longer would Highbury folk be subjected to Tottenham's favourite chant *3–1, We beat the scum 3–1.* They had an equally derisive riposte. *Two years, we only waited two years, and now the scum are in tears . . .* It's a charming rivalry.

'Avenger Adams', headlined the *Daily Express,* and George Graham described him as his hero. Now, Tony shies away from such glorifying praise, preferring to look at the wider picture. 'It was fabulous, for everyone and, I think, fitting after the first semi-final. One each was fair as far as Arsenal and Tottenham were concerned. It was nice to square things up after only two years' pain, to get that out the way was great, so all of North London could be happy. They'd given us a good hiding and we gave them a good hiding back. All done, thank you very much.'

As Sheffield Wednesday dispose of United in the other semi-final, English football has the unique scenario of two clubs contesting both domestic Cup Finals. So did it ever cross Arsenal minds that winning one apiece would be the decent outcome? Putting this to Tony he couldn't look more astonished if I'd asked him to run down Tottenham High Road starkers. 'What are you talking about! It's the Arsenal, it's George Graham, you wally! Oh dear, oh dear. What a thing to say, *we'll win a Cup each*. We want them all! Of course we do. We want them all and we want them all now.'

The Coca-Cola Cup Final is billed as the dress rehearsal, before the real thing in May. Still, victory earns the winners a place in Europe and offers the opportunity to become the only team in English football to clean up the Cups. First blood to Arsenal. Stephen Morrow snaffles the winner, his first goal for the club, but his ecstasy slips to agony during the post-match celebrations. Unsung heroes are usually soon forgotten outside the confines of the club they serve, but Morrow's bizarre Wembley experience is written into football folklore. Cavorting on the pitch, the captain picks up the scorer with such vigour he falls, landing awkwardly on the turf, and the young Irishman's arm is shattered. He leaves the field on a stretcher, face encased in an oxygen mask, and Tony is so distraught he needs coaxing to collect the trophy and after the match he goes straight home. 'I obviously felt gutted for Steve but if you asked him honestly, he was very, very pleased that he scored that goal at that particular moment in that particular game. I said to him when he was in hospital, "You'll be more known for that, Steve." That's the way it works I'm afraid. He didn't exactly turn round and thank me for it but it's true. It was his moment in time. That can't be taken away so we shouldn't have been sad even though for that night it wasn't the best. It wasn't right for me to go out and be happy in those circumstances. A few of the boys did, I had a restaurant booked, and I should have enjoyed it but it wasn't to be. I know it was a freak accident and I take some responsibility for it. But I've seen that done a million times.' He pauses, then adds in a sardonic voice, with a knowing smile, 'If we could go back we'd change it, wouldn't we, but we can't.'

The FA Cup Final is also decided by an unsung hero, but not until Arsenal and Wednesday complete a gruelling four hours of football. Fatigue plays the major role in what is widely advertised as the English game's prestigious 'showpiece', and having played five matches in ten days to complete their league fixtures the teams are harangued for producing a torpid draw. So it's back to Wembley for a replay, and the faithful from Highbury and Hillsborough dig deep into their pockets to finance a fourth visit in six weeks to the overpriced Venue of Legends.

In a torrential downpour on a bleak Thursday evening, the players dig deep into their spirit to create a far more compelling game. Arsenal, as ever, emanate immutable belief in their pursuit of silverware, and Wednesday make nonsense of their reputation as an outwardly pretty team with no inner backbone, particularly when Mark Bright breaks Andy Linighan's nose with a violent elbow. Wright scores his 15th Cup goal of the season to give Arsenal the advantage, only for Waddle to contrive an equaliser which deflects off Dixon's leg. And so these adversaries, who know each other so well they are almost inseparable, march on together into the monumental struggle of extra-time. Penalties beckon. There seems no other way of disconnecting the two sides. Mentally, everyone prepares for sudden death. In injury time John Jensen has a brainstorm and in a moment of madness, quite out of character, he blasts a shot on target. But it's deflected for a corner. Merson floats the ball into the box for Linighan, who poetically rises above Bright to thunder a header goalwards, broken nose and all . . . Chris Woods gets his hands to it but his wrists give way and the ball sails upwards into the roof of the net. It's a knockout.

Bob Wilson, in his customary position behind the goal, loses it completely. 'When Andy scored I jumped up with my arms in the air, umbrella flying,' he recalls. 'I was there as the Arsenal goalkeeping coach, and David is up there at the other end, and he's vying with Chris Woods for the England spot. I felt desperately sorry to see Chris drop it in but my man was a winner. We won the Cup. Chris Waddle, who was facing me and shell-shocked, got really upset and made a gesture because he thought I was working for the BBC and should be impartial but I wasn't working because of my connections. I wrote him a letter and I think he understands now but at the time it was really nasty.'

Arsenal's Double achievement is unparalleled. Wednesday's anguish is unimaginable. 'I felt very sorry for the Sheffield people, obviously,' says Tony, 'Although I don't think Dave Seaman did because I think he's a United fan.' This time the celebrations go without a hitch. Whooping it up in front of the Arsenal fans Adams has one arm round Linighan's neck and the other pointing at his head, as if to say, *Look at him. Look what he's done.* The £1 million defender had taken heavy flak as he struggled to justify his fee up to then. 'I think Andy was amazing,' Tony eulogises. 'To come in and play the way he did, he was fabulous, really strong, determined. A lot of people had questioned his ability, including myself, but he really was inspirational. I think he was calmer than me in all the games. It was fitting for him to score because he was the strongest man on that pitch. I was so pleased because he's such a lovely guy. He's been fantastic to work with, a true professional and a funny, dry lad as well. He changed next to me every day at Colney and it was just a pleasure to hear him in the mornings. We loved the same old films and stuff. He deserved it and I've got the greatest admiration for him. Great player and a great bloke.'

Thanks to Linighan's late intervention, echoing Arsenal's timely traditions of old, the FA Cup Final was spared its first shoot-out. The purists whimsically wiped relieved brows as the old trophy was saved from the gimmicky glitz of a lottery. Still, praise for the winners was grudging and there were plenty of disgruntled mutterings at the lack of classical elegance on show. Attacks on Arsenal's style cut little ice with the players. 'You can't knock it, we put two cups on the sideboard,' chirps Tony. 'You cannot knock success. You can try to, but you can't – it's that simple. We won two trophies out of three that year. George instilled a belief in us and it worked. My manager wanted me to play a certain way, it brought us success, and I believed in what we were doing. If you've got that belief it goes a hell of a long way. George is a realist and the players we had could not play the way we do now under Arsène Wenger – they weren't capable. We'd have made ourselves look silly and would probably have ended up bottom of the table. I always remember George came in one day when we'd not been performing. We all got carried away with ourselves and thought we were better than we were and he told us: "Look, you're very, very average players and don't forget it." I think he went a bit over the top.' Tony hoots with laughter.

An FA Cup-winners' medal completed Adams's domestic collection. 'It was a necessity,' he says. 'I needed everything, it was the most important thing in my life. Yes, Tony wanted everything. We all want recognition for our achievements – that's only human. You're a liar if you say you don't, so when you've got a trophy lifted above your head and you've reached your aim, it's a great buzz, a great fix. I loved every moment of it. Maybe I would have enjoyed it more now knowing how difficult it bloody well was. At the time it was so easy. You go from game to game and before you know it you've come out the other side and won all the trophies.

'Now, I've changed so much. I still want to win more trophies, and I'm going to do everything in my power as a professional footballer to try to do so, but if I don't, I don't. I can cope with that now. Before, it was the only thing, I *had* to win those trophies, do-or-die stuff. People like to put you in a box of being that type of person. I think I'm a genuine, honest guy who does his best to win for me and for Arsenal Football Club, because they employ me. If people view that as do-or-die, then it's do-or-die.'

Would you have taken a penalty, Tony, if it had come to that at Wembley? 'I'm pretty relaxed about penalties. As far as I'm concerned, the job's done, it's over, and whoever wins that it's like tossing a coin. But I'll do the best I can and I've got no fear. At Sampdoria I took one because everyone else bottled out. If you start to look at the fear of that then you're not players. I said, "Go on, make a name for yourself. You never know, you might be a hero. Are you too afraid of being a failure not to be a hero? You've just got to go and kick it, go and smack it, do your best." Mine actually came off the side of my boot and went in. If I missed it, I missed it. Don't carry that baggage around for the rest of your life. Just do your best.'

★

When he captained England during Euro 96 the rest of the country finally caught on to what it is about Tony Adams that makes him such a colossus. Such is his stature in the three-lioned shirt it seems mindboggling to remember how he was berated as a young buck when England were crushed in the 1988 European Championship, how he spent two years in international exile, how he was scorned by fans throughout the land. Whatever the obstacle, Adams finds the power to overcome. It's as if his career has been played out on a snakes-and-ladders board: after each elevation comes the slippery pitfall, and every time he prevails. This in itself takes fortitude. Add the full glare of the media and you really need to be made of sturdy stuff. Tony has grown up in public. Like pop darlings or film starlets, every twist is scrutinised. Unlike pop darlings and film starlets, Tony has to deal with *Schadenfreude*, the fact that people get a kick out of seeing him fall, and he has to meet a critical crowd of thousands, face to face, every week. Multiply this pressure by the Arsenal factor and the success factor, two elements guaranteed to invite a bitter tone, and it's clear Adams's ability to surmount barriers is remarkable.

That is why 7,500 Arsenal supporters converged upon Highbury for a reserve game against Reading in 1991 to welcome him home after two months in prison for drink driving. For years they had seen him overcome struggles for Arsenal on their behalf and now they wanted to pay him back so he could overcome a struggle of his own. At the end of the match Tony let it all out with an emotional roar of release so thunderous it drowned out the cheers of thousands.

George Graham recalls how kneejerk reactions called for the club to renounce Adams. 'We had all the media jumping in and fans writing in saying, "This is not the Arsenal way, Herbert Chapman would have had him slung out." Utter nonsense. Herbert Chapman had problem boys just like I had problem boys. Alex James, who was the greatest player ever, was continually going over the top with alcohol. Player's don't change.' Oh, but they do.

Sometimes Tony looks back in amazement at the man he once was. 'It just seems so far away, like a different person. Who was that guy? That's taking no desire from the man who sits here now, he still wants to achieve the same things, still keeps setting himself goals all the time. I think the minute you achieve everything in life you're ready for death. There's no point in living if you can't keep on pushing, having dreams, we all need them.'

The captain has turned renaissance man. As a player he's discovered new freedom of expression, as a person he's open-minded and constantly challenging his own opinions, and as a professional he's developed a more sensitive style of leadership – more gentle persuasion and a meaningful look than crude invective and clenched fists.

There's a popular myth that Arsène Wenger 'unshackled' Tony Adams. Not so. Tony Adams unshackled Tony Adams. 'I've done what I wanted to do,' he says. 'I'm playing without any fear and I'm trying to enjoy it. He's let me get on with it.' Long may it continue. 'That would be cool.' Arsenal want him to go on and on. He's been around for 18 years since signing schoolboy forms in 1979, and they've pretty much warmed to his presence by now. 'I think it's impossible not to form a kind of bond,' believes Tony. 'Even if they don't like you, if you're around for long enough, you stick, don't ya.' He chortles away. 'The future looks pretty good to me, I'm very optimistic at the moment and I can only see good times ahead.'

Nil

DAVID SEAMAN

Arsenal 1 Parma 0
4 May 1994

Seaman, Dixon, Winterburn, Davis, Bould, Adams, Campbell,
Morrow, Smith, Merson (McGoldrick), Selley

Underneath his moustache David Seaman wears a grin as vast as
his huge goalie hands. A Champion in his first season, a miserly
18 goals conceded, he soaks up the adulation of the Arsenal faithful as they herald a season of unmatched magnitude from the
man between the sticks. It's a significant moment, not least
because the day he joined the club he was the Highbury public's
enemy number one.

His predecessor John Lukic was a cult hero, you see, and a
good goalkeeper to boot, and on transfer deadline day in 1990,
when newspapers revealed George Graham was trying to pack
him off to QPR in exchange for Seaman, the fans were up in
arms. Being a stubborn lad, Lukic dug his heels in at Highbury
and refused to go, and his supporters roared to his defence. What
was so special about this David Seaman anyway? They didn't
want him, they wanted Johnny, and they made sure George knew
exactly how they felt, chorusing *We all agree Lukic is better then
Seaman!* every game until the season's end.

When it comes to being headstrong, Graham has few peers
and his mind was made up. He had picked the brains of Bob
Wilson for an opinion on the QPR man, who pronounced,
'Potentially he will be one of the great goalkeepers.' George asked

164

if he was sure. 'I'm as sure as I'll ever be,' added Bob, profoundly. That was it. The manager would buy his chosen number one in the summer, the dissenting voices would soon come round, and if Johnny didn't like it, he could sample life in the reserves or he could leave. Not that George was a control freak or anything. Nor was it a case of holding Arsenal's net minder in low esteem. He valued Lukic amongst the top six goalkeepers in the country. But he simply rated Seaman as the best.

David's transfer was an absurdly protracted affair. In fact it took six years from first attempt to eventual success. He almost joined in 1984 from Peterborough but ended up in Birmingham after Lukic again declined to be a bargaining tool and fought for his Highbury rights. 'If John had gone to Birmingham I would have gone to Arsenal from Peterborough – that's how long it's been going on,' sighs David. 'Then, with the transfer deadline move falling through, I was really sick. But I knew within a few days that I was still going to be signing.' During the close-season Seaman arrived, Lukic departed for Leeds, and the fans whinged. As welcomes go, they greeted their new keeper with the kind of suspicion granted to unfamiliar folk who walk into a cosy local pub where they don't easily take to strangers. Prickly moments for David. 'It was good to finally turn up although I was quite nervous because I'd heard the stories about the fans supporting John. I just felt I wanted to get in there to show the Arsenal fans what I could do.'

The Gooners used to have this ritual with Lukic. It was an imaginative variation on the chant-a-player's-name-and-he'll-wave-at-you theme. From behind his goal they sang *Johnny do the twist*, which he acknowledged with a dainty bum wiggle. They cheered heartily. Oh, the simple pleasures of life. David's first opportunity to win over the Lukic fan club came in a quiet, quaint Swedish town where 30-odd Arsenal aficionados who accompanied the team on their pre-season Scandinavian tour tested him out with a burst of *Seaman do the twist*. He glanced curiously at this motley crew. What on earth were they on about? 'Johnny used to do it all the time,' they explained, gyrating furiously. David obliged. He was in. Still, 30 fanatics so daft they dared not miss even a summer friendly did not make a North

Bank. 'My first game in England was against Wolves in a friendly and I still got a mixed reception when I went out,' David remembers. 'But I made a few saves and after the game I walked over to them and kissed the badge and everything. They loved it.' He giggles away.

Pleasure turned to sheer delight immediately with that Championship season in 1991. 'It was such a great achievement words can't describe how it felt,' remarks David. 'My motivation for leaving QPR was to win things. When I finish my career, I want something to look back at medalwise. I want to look back and say, *We won this and that's what I've got.* Money doesn't come into it when you're talking about stuff like that. I had a choice of Arsenal or Manchester United, and Ray Wilkins, who was a team-mate at QPR, told me, "Go to Arsenal because you'll win trophies with them straight away." He was right. The main difference which struck me was the level of expectancy. We are expected to win something every season, otherwise it's a failure. When I was at QPR I didn't feel that; it was just a case of making sure you stay in the First Division. Could I cope with these big pressures every game? That's what I wanted to find out.' Were there any times you didn't cope, David? 'Er, no, not really.' He smiles broadly.

He couldn't be more laid-back if he had a bed placed in his goalmouth. This mellow temperament keeps him ice cool in the heat of battle. Yet beneath this relaxed, unflappable demeanour lies the heart of a true competitor. While some keepers show their spirit with demented dives and brave leaps and wild rantings – Bob Wilson was one – others conceal their simmering spirit behind a cool, composed exterior, à la Pat Jennings. 'David is like Pat, absolute God-given ability,' believes Bob. 'And he's got a brain, like Pat, that works out what's good for him. Why go diving down risking having your ear torn off or punctured lungs like I did? David's had broken ribs but he's such an incredible winner. It's different strokes for different folks. David Seaman knows exactly what is required.'

Goalkeeping is all about confidence and David has an endless supply on tap, which ensures he's never intimidated by playing such a sensitive position. It's a keeper's lot that he will occasionally be beaten, however eminent he is, and if every goal batters his confidence he's finished. David's faith in his own supremacy keeps him nerveless. That's how he recovered from the shock of once conceding double figures in 45 minutes. 'It was my first game for my junior school and I came in for the second half and let in 14 goals,' he confesses. 'We lost 26–0.'

★

In inscribing the name of Arsenal on the 1993 FA Cup George Graham completed the rare feat of winning every honour in the English game as a player and a manager. On display in his study the Stroller also had a European prize from the 1970 Fairs Cup triumph. Success in Europe was the one omission on his managerial CV. It was a bugbear, and one he aimed to squash. George made no apologies for setting his sights on the 1994 Cup-Winners' Cup before the season began and if the domestic competitions had to be subordinate issues, so be it. The players were less inclined to prioritise – 'You can't do that,' suggests Seaman – but Europe was George's grail. Arsenal had proved themselves on English soil and the time had come to conquer the Continent.

He had only had one crack at Europe. Succumbing to Benfica in the European Cup hurt deeply and George was on a mission to make amends. 'We got blitzed out of it,' recalls David. 'It made us feel that if that's the sort of standard we have to get to, then we'll get to it, but at the time we were nowhere near.' Some pundits believed the team were no nearer next time they got the map and pins out at Highbury. 'It's hard to believe Arsenal will be playing on the same planet, let alone in the same competition, as Parma,' voiced *The Guardian*. As if to emphasise the chasm, the Italians had won the Cup-Winners' Cup with panache at Wembley the week before Arsenal slogged it out on the same turf to claim the FA Cup against Sheffield Wednesday. Food for thought.

Arsenal are in illustrious company in the European draw. The might of Real Madrid, Ajax, Torino, Paris Saint-Germain and Ferencvaros also inhabit the Parma universe which the Gunners strive to rocket towards. And there is one other club in the hat boasting vast European pedigree: Benfica. Arsenal yearn to level an old score against the team who had taught them such a harsh lesson in 1991. Their naïvety against the Portuguese giants had made a firm impression on George and his reaction is to make caution, patience and organisation Cup-Winners' Cup watchwords. Others interpret that as boring, but George is confident he can have the last laugh.

The lads soon see just how focused he is on Europe. Key players are rested before Cup-Winners' Cup games either to guard against injury or to confuse visiting scouts. The result? Moderate league form. But it has the desired European effect. After disposing of Odense of Denmark in the first round Standard Liège are bombarded 3–0 at home and 7–0 away, a record scoreline. The goalfest in Belgium is even more astonishing considering it is achieved without Ian Wright, sacrificed because of a yellow card picked up against Odense – perish the thought he should miss a more important tie by collecting another booking. Still, seven goals? Food for thought for the critics who dubbed George's boys *Arsenil*. Perhaps they were referring to the defence?

Seaman needed binoculars in Liège to keep track of the match. The ball rarely entered his half let alone his box. Surely a goalkeeper enjoys such occasions. 'They are the hardest games,' he says. 'You've got nothing to do then all of a sudden you might get a shot and it might be the one save you've got to make. If you're not ready for it you can get crucified by it. That's the hard part of goalkeeping, keeping your concentration while the ball is at the other end. It might be like that until the 89th minute and then you're called upon to make that one, all-important save. That's what international football is like. The main worry in Europe comes from the teams you don't know. There's a fear of a freak result when you don't know anything about them, but once you get past those stages we've got a better chance. When it gets to the big games like Torino and Paris Saint-Germain, we know what we have to do. It was then that we realised what European football is all about.'

George is meticulous in his preparation for foreign forays, studying videos and scouting reports with the dedication of a professor, plotting tactical manoeuvres with the deliberation of a chess master. Once he'd taken an educated guess on the opposition's strategy, he set up a shadow game with the reserves imitating, say, Torino's style of play so the team could work on ways to counter it. George is particularly concerned about the threat of floating striker Enzo Francescoli and roaming midfielder Benito Carbone, so two of the young lads are instructed to meander all over the place in training. Ominously, the pseudo-Italian reserves beat the first team. George warns, 'If you give them that much room they'll tear you apart.' So it's off to the video room for the players to sit through the latest Torino blockbuster. Watch and learn.

There are mental as well as tactical disciplines to adapt to in Europe. The manager preaches the benefits of patience, so his players can find the right moment to apply the killer touch, and self-control, so they can cope with the frustration of frequent shirt-pulling and crafty intimidation, hidden from the referee's eye but designed to provoke the players. Out in Italy, a handful of travelling fans try, on behalf of the team, to get retaliation in first. Having a drink in the Torino team's hotel, they approach giant striker Andrea Silenzi under the auspices of seeking an autograph. 'Tony Adams is gonna murder you,' they smile. Silenzi smiles back, blissfully unaware. 'No chance,' they say sympathetically to Francescoli. He twitches. During the game neither gets a look in.

With the impassable presence of Adams and Bould at the back, the tireless snapping of Hillier and Jensen in midfield, Arsenal out-Italian Torino, content simply to nullify their threat. It's described in *The Times* as 'highly organised tedium'. It's no classic but George is thrilled with the 0–0 scoreline. The job is completed at Highbury in the style set to become a blueprint for success in Europe: another clean sheet for Seaman and a set-piece goal, thanks to a cultured delivery from Davis and a glancing header from Adams. One-nil to the Arsenal. A signature tune is born. The lyrics are oddly appropriate for the club – it's a little idiosyncrasy amongst Arsenal fans that they cherish the prag-matic as much as the romantic. No other club gets such a buzz out of sneaking results, out of winning in a way which rankles with the knockers. Yawn if you must, snipe if you will, we'll take the trophies thanks very much.

The semi-finals offer a mouthwatering prospect. Not only are Arsenal still going strong in the competition but so are Benfica, and the two clubs are kept apart in the draw. The potential for George's dream final is still on and the word 'destiny' is bandied about in the pubs of N5. Another factor wistfully prophesied over the umpteenth jar is John Jensen scoring a goal in the final. If it's going to happen anywhere it's bound to happen in his home town of Copenhagen. Perfect. All we have to do is stifle Paris Saint-Germain, nick a goal, and we're there.

Arsenal travel to France and defy every expectation. First surprise: the Gunners abandon their customary caution. Although they remain defensively careful, they attack with cutting venom, frightening the life out of the French. Second shock: Jensen comes closer than ever to his first goal in almost two years in Arsenal colours with a scorching piledriver which Bernard Lama incredibly pushes onto a post. Seaman jests at the memory. 'What, didn't he hit the stands? It was funny, he was even shocking in training and when he used to score he celebrated like he'd scored in a game. It was good fun but John Jensen had other qualities he put into the side other than his goalscoring.' This is possibly the Dane's finest performance for the club, bossing midfield with animated vigour, which frees Davis to provide the subtle touch. His beautifully flighted free-kick is headed home by a jubilant Wright. *One-nil to the Arsenal* . . . Third bolt out of the blue: after four consecutive clean sheets in Europe the lads concede a goal. David Ginola flicks a near-post corner past Seaman. 'What annoyed me is that sometimes teams have a defender on each post and if I'd had someone on that near post they would have headed it away,' he rues. David is a perfectionist who analyses every goal he concedes to see how he can improve, to make him more determined. Nevertheless, Arsenal take heart from the fact that Lama has a far more nervewracking night's work than Seaman.

Normal service is resumed at Highbury for the second leg with that groundhog scoreline, 1–0. Campbell steers a header home and Adams and co are Trojans, keeping PS-G's counter-attacks at bay. Arsenal pulsates to the new theme tune and the night air crackles with excitement. Suddenly the exuberant Wright, chasing irrepressibly, lunges into a late tackle. He is shown his second yellow card of the campaign and will miss the final. The emotional striker cannot hold back the tears. In the dressing-room at half-time, the lads try to lift him – he still has a job to do to ensure Arsenal make it even if he won't. 'He was totally distraught,' remembers David. 'It was a terrible feeling for him, one of the horrible sides of football. We were just saying, "*Come on, Ian, just get us to the final.*" He was all right.'

Wright has to put the good of the team above his own personal pain. In Copenhagen, David will have to do the same, playing through the agony of a broken rib so the team can benefit from the experience and reassurance their number one man provides, injured or not. 'I got that at QPR a week before the final from Bradley Allen, who must have been the thinnest player on the pitch,' he says. 'It was a bouncing ball coming though, I went up and he just stuck his elbow in there. Straight away I thought, *Oh no.* I could just tell. It's happened to me twice since, that exact same feeling, and that's what started it all off.' Voice full of mock menace, he adds, 'I'm still waiting to meet him again . . .'

For the Cup-Winners' Cup Final, he will require six painkilling injections to numb the nerves around that cracked rib. David's injury is just part of a disastrous build-up for Arsenal. Martin Keown and David Hillier, Graham's first and second choices for a midfield marking role, both fail fitness tests, falling into a black hole in the middle of the team which has already claimed John Jensen. The devastated Dane had dreamt one night about breaking his Arsenal duck in Copenhagen, but failed to foresee the nightmare of violent knee ligament damage sustained playing for his country three weeks before the final. Ian Selley and Stephen Morrow, each with fewer than 50 appearances under his belt, slot into midfield and need to play the game of their lives. At least Paul Davis is fit and in favour. For almost two years George had confined him to the Highbury wilderness before reinstating the one midfielder with artistic touch and vision on Arsenal's books and his influence shone through the Cup-Winners' Cup run. On him so much would depend as playmaker.

But who to prompt in the absence of Ian Wright – the man whose strike-rate that season provided almost as many goals as the rest of the team put together? The pundits reckoned Arsenal were a one-man show and questioned where the winner would

171

come from without him. 'People did say stop Wrighty and you'll stop Arsenal and to an extent that was true,' admits Alan Smith. 'He would finish up with 30 goals but we'd be very low on the goalscoring charts as a team. We were so one-dimensional going forward and I think that was to the detriment of our overall game. That's something George didn't really rectify, he was there four years with Wrighty and he didn't buy a winger or a creative midfielder to put his foot on the ball, which he should have done.'

So, one-track-minded Arsenal face the final deprived of their spearhead, robbed of brute strength in midfield, and nursing their keeper. With the exception of captain Tony Adams, the spine of the team is damaged from top to bottom. In contrast, Nevio Scala's Parma, who disposed of Benfica in their semi-final, are a finely tuned side who are injury-free, defending their Cup-Winners' Cup crown, and oozing an air of sophisticated superiority. 'When they've got Zola and Asprilla and Brolin dropping deep you do think *How are we going to cope?*' recalls Smith. 'I think George was worried. He didn't want to get embarrassed in a showpiece final after we'd done so well to get there, and he probably showed more anxiety before that game than usual. But by that stage most of us were so experienced: David, the back four, Davo, myself, Merse, and Kevin to a degree. We thought, "Stop panicking, George. What's he panicking about? We'll be all right."'

4 May. Arsenal v Parma. Cup-Winners' Cup Final. Hans Christian Andersen's Copenhagen is the City of Fantasy. Twenty thousand tourists from North London charge into the Danish capital to indulge their romantic reveries. From the second they arrive, they bawl *One nil to the Arsenal* incessantly; it hangs in the air like an echo, ricocheting off every bar, every hotel, every restaurant, every street corner. The locals warm to the theme. In one hostelry a hulking blond Viking watches in awe as a merry red-and-white band have a sing-song. He wants to make friends. 'Hello,' he says, 'I'm a seaman. I'm from Finland.' *Sea-maaan! Sea-maaan!* they yell. It's a sign! He looks utterly bemused. 'Goalkeeper. Football. Number One,' they explain. Everyone shakes hands and clinks glasses.

The fear factor which accompanies English football fans abroad is lost in a Copenhagen carnival. 'It was one big foamy party and only good natured: an enormous skinhead apologised when he bumped into me,' wrote a surprised Danish journalist, chronicling the street scenes which preceded the game. The only hairy moment comes when a fire breaks out in Burger King. The cause, it transpires, is excessive British eating habits rather than hooligan behaviour – never before had a chip-fryer been under such pressure to spontaneously combust. The Gooners clear the road and cheer as the fire engine draws up. Well, they want more chips. Meanwhile, the Parma supporters are nowhere to be seen. There aren't many in town.

The party continues in the Parken. With its classy, symmetrical red stands, and with the Arsenal army outnumbering their Italian counterparts by three to one, it's a real home from Highbury home. 'The amount of Arsenal fans there was amazing,' gasps David. 'They were everywhere. They weren't just in one section, they were behind the goal, down both sides and even in the Italian end.' George's boys are visibly boosted, and any glimmer of an advantage is essential to help them to topple the favourites. Even competition organisers UEFA, it seems, can't see beyond a Parma victory. 'I'll always remember, when we pulled up in the coach just before the game, they had the European Cup-Winners' Cup podium ready to bring on after the game to present the trophy. It had Parma written on it,' exclaims David. 'All the lads went, *Bloody hell, we can't believe this. Right, we'll bloody show them.* It was strange to see it, though. They must have had Arsenal as well to stick over, but there it was with the date on it and all the UEFA paraphernalia, and Parma. They painted that on first.'

As Arsenal well know, character *can* triumph over adversity. To pep up mental strength Adams revs the motivation machine, to perk up physical strength Gary Lewin the physio goes into overdrive, strapping and massaging and injecting. Seaman is the very important patient. 'I had four injections before I went out for my warm-up and two more at half-time because they started wearing off,' says David. 'There had been some doubt as to whether I should play, but once I'd had the injections I knew I could. Gary and the doctor had said, "You won't feel anything when we've injected you." That was it. The pain had gone and it was out of my mind as well.' He affords himself no additional shield in the form of bandages or supports – the only extra protection comes in the shape of his trusted back four.

It's daring hearts against dancing feet, and Parma's rapid, fluent movement threatens Arsenal from the off. Brolin arcs a free header over the bar, then angles a shot against the post. Did you have it covered, David? 'Obviously,' he smiles. Up the other end Smith is concerned, *Oh no, we're going to get hammered here . . .* But within an instant it is he who supplies the hammer blow. Lee Dixon lofts a cross into the heart of the Parma box, Minotti makes a hash of a vain overhead kick clearance – 'What's he done that for?' quizzes Smudger – and Arsenal's number 9 cushions the ball on his chest and volleys in off the post. 'Great goal but it was a surprise it went in,' recalls Seaman. 'I didn't really expect the goalie to get beat from there. I know it was near post and the ball swerved, but being on the pitch and watching it I wasn't too sure it had gone in until I saw Alan reeling away with his arms up and everything, telling everyone to *COME ON!* '

They had been singing it lustily all day. They had been singing it from the moment they arrived in the ground. They had been singing it while the game was scoreless . . . Now the refrain has new meaning. *ONE-NIL TO THE ARSENAL!* How predictable can you get? 'We knew the fans were just waiting for us to score and as soon as we did, straight away that song came out. It was a good feeling,' says David. Above all, the song is a testimony to the team's unbreakable defence. The attackers find it ever so slightly patronising but for the men at the back, it is a source of pride. 'Always a good defence, that's what they say,' crows David. Scoring was always going to be the trickiest task and now it's a case of hanging on for all of 70 minutes. Smith had provided the one and Seaman has to keep his side of the bargain and keep the nil: 'It wasn't so much *I* as *we*. I need the four in front of me to do their stuff as well and they did it perfectly. It was backs to the wall, one-way traffic, but Parma didn't really have too many clear-cut chances after that. That was the one time I really enjoyed the offside rule. We were just holding the box and every time they

174

were running in they were getting caught offside. It was great. We knew that on paper they had a better-looking side than us in terms of talent but we knew in ourselves that if we got the goal we could defend it, which was exactly what happened on the night.'

The risk of playing wounded soldier Seaman pays the ultimate dividend when he plucks a save of marvellous quality to deflect a fireball from Zola away from the danger zone as the miracle of anaesthetic works its magic. 'Too right,' he winces. 'And it was on the right-hand side which was the side I'd done my ribs as well. Because he's got such little feet and quick legs, he can strike it and it doesn't look like he's hit it really hard but I knew it was really travelling. Still, the pain wasn't there so I just flung my arm up and got a good touch on it.

'When we flew home one of the club doctors came and sat next to me for half an hour and I was thinking, *What's he sat there for?* Apparently he was making sure I was all right because of the amount of stuff they had put in me – there could have been a few complications with the pressure of the plane. They didn't tell me this until after. But I was allowed to have champagne – straight away in the dressing-room.' Cue giggles.

The misty-eyed masses witness one of Arsenal's finest hours: a triumph named desire. Out comes the UEFA podium, hastily prepared for the club who, as they say, wanted it more. Out hobbles John Jensen, who is given a raucous welcome. Out bounds Wrighty, who floats round the pitch like an uncaged bird. He is elated the boys have finally scotched the hype about Arsenal's reliance on him. 'It's not a one-man-team thing,' he claims. 'At the start the players would have a laugh about it but people got a bit resentful after a while because it wasn't nice. I used to do everything I could to play that down. Okay, my job is to score goals, but we're still all Arsenal. That's why I was so happy when we won the Cup-Winners' Cup Final. People had been saying: "You won't win because you're suspended." We *did* win. And it was a typical Arsenal performance without me there. I was disappointed not to play but I got my medal, I played up to the final, and we won it.' Over in Italy, Arsenal's victory made an impression on a player watching events on television. His name was Dennis Bergkamp.

That song keeps Copenhagen awake all night long. After a while, the art of conversation surrenders to its charms. Fans lose the ability to speak, communicating only through simple melody. As long as it scans the tune it is all right. *Would you like another beer?* for example. It's entrenched so deeply in everyone's psyche they can hear it for days afterwards, humming through the aeroplane air-conditioning, droning through the rhythm of the tube, chiming in the running bath. One-nil to the Arsenal. Wonderful, wonderful . . . Are we all a goalkeeper short of a full team?

★

Seaman, Dixon, Adams, Bould, Winterburn. It's a legendary defensive unit which has proved itself to be the finest back line in the English game for the best part of a decade. It's unlikely football will ever see their likes again. 'The way the game is going at the moment, there will be a lot of changes and players on shorter contracts, so groups won't be at clubs long enough to achieve what we have,' says David. 'The Arsenal defence becomes even more well known every year. We have the fewest goals conceded most seasons. George used to do quite a lot of defensive training, where the midfielders and the attackers would have a go at us. We kept them out, surprise, surprise.' He beams. 'By playing so many games together with Lee, Tony, Steve and Nigel, a natural understanding develops. Plus we have a good rapport. That's the good thing about Arsenal: no one's too big, no one gets above everybody else. As soon as someone starts, the lads are straight on your case, bringing you back to earth.'

For David, European success took him to a higher plane. Since Peter Shilton's international retirement he had been in a three-horse race against Chris Woods and Tim Flowers for his country's number one shirt, and a succession of shut-outs in the Cup-Winners' Cup strengthened Seaman's case. Three goals conceded and six clean sheets in nine games offered irrevocable evidence. 'At that time I was making a serious challenge for the England jersey, so for me it was important to play in Europe and against the top European players,' he explains. 'It was something new and I wanted to see how I coped with it. There is big pressure in domestic games, and the next stage up, the European games, brings even more pressure, and then . . . there's the England games.'

Arsenal's Cup-Winners' Cup defence the following season brought David even more experience of those pressures: from the semi-final against Sampdoria, when he was hailed as the hero after a stunning hat-trick of penalty saves, to the final against Real Zaragoza, when he was unkindly labelled the villain for being beaten by a gobsmacking goal from Nayim. According to Bob Wilson, it's how you learn from the spinning coin of goalkeeping – pleasure on one side, peril on the other – which builds you. 'In the final he made one of the truly great saves from Esnaider when he knocked it onto the post and made a double save, but the only thing people remember is the Nayim goal. He accepts that – but people who know realise Arsenal wouldn't have got to the final without him. It's one of those things: you win some, you lose some, you've got to take it. I will say to my dying day the Nayim goal wasn't an error by David Seaman. I think he was in the perfect position for a through ball to Esnaider, which looked to be odds-on. Instead, Nayim tried something and it came off. David was always backpedalling and it was a foot under the bar and that was that. There are times when you get a bit shellshocked and he has this incredible ability to take it on his shoulders.'

David was lampooned in the aftermath of that astonishing strike at every stadium in the country. Opposition supporters taunted him, flapping their arms around as they sang *Nayim from the halfway line*. It fell on deaf ears. He mimed a theatrical yawn as if to congratulate them on their originality, painted mental pictures of all his prizes, and continued smiling under the moustache. 'All I think of is my medals,' he says. 'That's my biggest comeback, having a look at all my medals and my caps. You've got to live it to the maximum when you get the highs. You've got to really milk it for everything – you might not be there again. When you're up there you know just round the corner can be a downer, as we all know. And when you have your downs you remember the ups.' Since Euro 96, funnily enough, opposition fans no longer flap and they even serenade David with a new song: *England's number one*.

Wonderland

DENNIS BERGKAMP

Arsenal 3 Tottenham 1
24 November 1996

Lukic, Dixon, Winterburn, Keown, Bould, Adams, Platt, Wright,
Merson, Bergkamp, Vieira

Unveiling their new signing to the press pack, Arsenal screen an anthology of his goals, just in case the scribes aren't familiar with the footballer sitting before them. The star attraction cocks his head to glance at the film rolling behind him as the soundtrack starts to play. The Stone Roses strum their guitars along to his greatest hits . . . *This is the one, this is the one we waited for . . .* We waited all right. Fifteen years. In 1980 we lost Liam Brady and we waited, and waited, and we had success, but we never had that rare aura of sporting genius in our midst. Not until Arsenal's shopping expedition at one of Brady's old clubs brought the genuine article back to Highbury. This is the one. Arsenal, like every other football team he had ever played for, were counting on Dennis Bergkamp.

Ever since he was a 16-year-old débutant introduced to the world by Johan Cruyff, people expected him to be some kind of miracle-worker. Ajax did, casting him as the fulcrum of all their hopes. Internazionale did, viewing him as the single solution to their multitude of problems. Arsenal did, longing for him to spirit the club into a more beautiful future. His presence alone inspired a mood of awed reverence. With his pick of the world's clubs, Dennis Bergkamp actually chose to come to Highbury.

Just thinking about it was tantamount to some hedonistic, hallucinogenic trip. Discovering it was reality filled Arsenal hearts with grovelling gratitude.

Even his team-mates were thankful. It's customary for all newcomers to make a speech to the squad and they sat in respectful silence as Dennis orated: 'I came to Arsenal not just to have a change of direction in my career, I really want to achieve something and I hope to do well here. I just want to add something to the team and hopefully make a difference for the Championship.' Instead of the usual ripple of applause, the players flung their arms in the air and wailed *We are not worthy!* Dennis blushes at the memory: 'As a joke they did that bowing from *The Life of Brian*. They had all sorts of jokes, and it's nice to have those things because it makes you feel at home.' Modest by nature, he doesn't fit the mould of your average football messiah. In spite of his celestial gifts he is an admirably grounded character. Dennis, like Monty Python's sacred parody Brian Cohen, is just an ordinary bloke thrust into deification. Blessed are the cheesemakers.

It was the crazed Italian intrusion into the Life of Dennis which hurried his departure from Serie A. Inter wanted him to right every wrong which beset them, and when they detected he was in fact a homo sapiens and not a god, they barracked him. They hemmed him in to the point of claustrophobia, so he didn't feel free to express himself on or off the field. Dennis sought a quieter existence, where he could work on his football and live his life on his own terms. And so to Arsenal: a big club with a family feel, a club he describes as simultaneously ambitious and relaxed, a club which doesn't simply want players to perform. It wants them to belong.

He still had to shoulder the treatment heaped upon him as the man who came to save Arsenal. 'People were acting like that but in a calmer, English way so I didn't feel any pressure,' he explains. 'Even when I didn't score everyone was telling me I was playing well. It was always so positive, which helped me a lot. People want you to do well and if you don't, okay, you're still a great player. That's what they say. That's nice. It was different in Italy where before every game they said, "Two goals today, eh?" What do they expect from me!' For Dennis the contrast was marked. From the Inter fans who loitered outside the training ground hissing threats that they would break his legs if he didn't produce, to the Arsenal fans who couldn't stop smiling inanely simply to see him in a red-and-white shirt and smothered him with goodwill.

Not everybody in North London extended a welcoming hand. Tottenham chairman Alan Sugar greeted Dennis's arrival with a vitriolic attack on overpriced, overpaid foreigners who unscrupulously regard the Premiership as a quick stop and a fast buck. Having been bitten by the Jürgen Klinsmann experience – the German illuminated White Hart Lane all too briefly – he depicted every import as a *Carlos Kickaball* who comes to England for a pretty penny only to leave after a season. 'Well, it didn't happen with Arsenal, it only happened with their team. Maybe he should blame himself,' Dennis remarks wryly. 'For me when I hear such a story – and the press come to me for a reaction – I can only talk about myself and I signed a four-year contract and didn't sign a four-year contract to leave after one year. That's my opinion. Maybe there are different foreigners with other opinions. For a start I never understand why people talk about other people when they don't really know them. Even when I played in Italy there were a lot of people who talked about me, then I read their names and thought, *Who is that? I never met them!* Old players, ex-players, talking about what I was doing and what I should do. They don't pick up the phone and call me. I can appreciate it if they do that, if they say, "I've played abroad and I did this, maybe it will help you . . ." That's better than putting it in the papers.' Dennis has a sceptic's eye for both criticism and praise if it's not from someone he knows and respects.

As an introvert, the intensity of the Italian press was a bane. He was hounded, and when he withdrew from their attentions they interviewed his gardener, or wrote that he was losing his hair. Although the English media is hardly renowned for its sensitivity, it was a comparative relief. 'A pleasant surprise,' he says. Nonetheless, the tabloids toyed with the possibility he might be a £7.5 million flop. Misfiring at lowly Hartlepool was reason enough for an early gibe and HARTLE-FOOL was emblazoned over the back pages. Failing to find the net in his first six Arsenal appearances prompted the *Daily Mirror* to publish a clock after each match, notching up all his goalless hours and minutes. The man himself was unabashed: 'For myself, six games is a long time, even if I don't see myself as the kind of striker who has to score every game. It was a long period but somehow I felt okay. I played well so it didn't really bother me. I lived in a hotel, I didn't read any papers, I was fine. The players were fine. The first time I really noticed that everyone was talking a lot about it was the moment that I scored my first goal. Then everybody was going, "Phew, it was a long time." I thought, *Oh. I didn't even know, thanks for telling me.*' He mimes an aghast expression then cracks into gentle laughter.

The fans were tangibly anxious for him to score – as much for him as for themselves – and when he buried a half-volley against Southampton their joy flowed out of the stands and into Dennis. That they were so happy for him warmed his soul: 'So many people were jumping up when I scored, they really wanted me to do well and that's an amazing feeling. And the way the players reacted, Ian Wright was on my neck, it was great. At that moment especially I felt I belonged.' What better way to enjoy such exhilaration than to present a self-made wonder goal minutes later, a meandering run and vicious bending shot which suggested his confidence was on the mend after the jolts inflicted in Serie A.

His first season was one of adaptation and consolidation and the signs promised greater days to come. The man who had won European medals with Ajax and Inter Milan crowned the campaign with another astounding strike to send Arsenal into raptures and into the UEFA Cup, the minimum requirement for a player of his stature. 'I feel it's normal for a top team to be in Europe,' he says. 'If we don't qualify, and we don't win anything, it's a lost season. It's something you need to do and I think I would have been really disappointed if we didn't get into Europe. Then to get a German team in the first round . . . maybe we'll get better luck next time.' Losing to Borussia Moenchengladbach was a bitter blow, such is the Dutch football rivalry with their neighbours. 'The Germans!' groans Dennis with a withering smile, lifting his eyes skywards.

★

Bergkamp's flashes of inestimable craft and intuitive vision were enough for Don Howe to assess him as a Rolls-Royce of a player and for Bob Wilson to claim his first touch was as good as Pele's. He was the pivot of the team, but there was the lingering opinion that you only get the best out of the central cog if the surrounding cogs function smoothly too. An improved midfield and perhaps a consistent winger or two would allow Dennis to bloom to his true potential. 'I wouldn't mind if the team was a little stronger so it's not really one person who stands out. It would be much better and maybe I can do better as well,' he reckoned. Changes in personnel during the summer would reveal to him the extent of Arsenal's aspirations.

But what nobody imagined was the most crucial change in personnel the club had in mind. A week before the big kick-off to season 1996–97, manager Bruce Rioch was sacked. Trying times for Dennis, a foreign player with only one year in England under his belt in the middle of a camp rocked by unrest and split about whether or not they agreed with the dismissal. The up-heaval vexed him. 'I didn't really see a reason why,' Dennis says. 'We started something off in my first year and I thought, *This year we can do better.* Especially after a disappointing European Championships for myself, I really was focused on doing well in the league. I felt it was a strange decision at that moment. I was very disappointed, I didn't know what was happening, what the plans were for the future. They fired someone who had the same ideas as I had. The ideas why I joined this club – the way he thought about playing attacking football and the way I played, for me it was the English game. Suddenly I felt maybe they want to go on another track, playing more defensive or go back to the old days. I thought, "What do I have to do with my future?"'

In appointing Arsène Wenger, the club are trying to create a future to suit Dennis to perfection. Arsenal's aim is to mesh the best aspects of English football with the finest elements of the European game. He now believes the French revolutionary paves the way for him and the club to fulfil their ambitions. 'It's a pity then that he wasn't there from the start. I still feel sympathy for

Bruce Rioch, but on the other hand we are doing well and progressing and I think this way we can achieve something.'

Contractual constraints meant the handover from one manager to the next was slipshod. To reactionary English eyes Arsène's selection was the worst-kept secret in the cosmos, a step into the great unknown, and a two-month lull while he completed his obligations in Japan was ridiculed. The board braced themselves, willing to ride rough terrain for those stormy few weeks as they were convinced he would drive Arsenal towards a sunny new landscape. Meanwhile, the team were guided by caretaker manager Stewart Houston then, when he left for QPR, by caretaker-caretaker manager Pat Rice. The tremendous unity within the squad defied the commotion off the field and not only kept Arsenal ticking over, but meant they were second in the table, and a single point off the top, when le gaffer arrived. The boys did the club, and themselves, proud.

'When I have stopped playing football and I look back, I think what I experienced that year, with all the problems and things that happened, it was incredible,' coos Dennis. 'At the time you get on with it and train the next day and play the next Saturday, no problem. But when you step back and look at it, it was an amazing time, and therefore it's amazing what we achieved that season. Every week there was someone in the tabloids with a different problem at the beginning of the season and we just kept going, kept winning. That's when you felt the team spirit. Sometimes you wondered, *Do we really need a manager?* because we kept on training the same way, everyone was focused. Normally, when there is no manager, especially with young players as I experienced with Ajax, everybody is not really training. The attitude is *Not today.* But the team just kept going, which was great.'

Wenger was worth waiting for. Herbert Chapman, Highbury's great visionary from the past, would approve of the way he set about modernising Arsenal, full of invigorating ideas and all introduced with a subtle, stylish touch. His blueprint encompasses the players' overall outlook on their working lives and their day-to-day routine has been completely redefined: stretching routines instead of stressed muscles, broccoli instead of burgers, a masseur, fitness coach and extra physio assimilated into the support staff to give the team every possible chance to perform at their physical peak.

Suddenly it's Dennis who is entirely at ease with the scene while the rest of the squad must adapt. 'It's European style of training, European methods, European thinking,' he says. 'That was no surprise to me, having played in Holland and Italy where it is normal. Everybody is now talking about diets and everything we have here.' He feigns a look of fascinated curiosity. 'It's a big story, that you have to pay attention to what you eat, and especially with the English lads, what you drink.' The consummate professional smiles, without a trace of condescension. In fact he finds it all quaintly engaging. 'The way they can drink is part of the English culture and you shouldn't take all that away. You should allow the players to have a drink or two when they want to, of course they can, but be more careful. It isn't a big deal to pay attention to your body when you are a professional footballer. They are used to it now and they aren't complaining.'

Wenger's philosophy on the field also encourages the players to embrace a more continental style. The Highbury chant of *Tony Adams on the wing* epitomises a new licence to thrill, and in Patrick Vieira, Arsenal's midfield hole, which gaped maddeningly for years, is filled. For too long the Gunners took the flyover instead of the scenic route, but the young Frenchman has a presence too good to be bypassed. In Arsenal's first game under Wenger at Blackburn, Vieira played a one-two out of defence, carried the ball through midfield, then released Ian Wright with a pinpoint pass. Goal.

It reminds Dennis of the ethos he was schooled in. 'Like the Ajax system, and what Arsenal is trying to do now, Patrick is a great example of that,' he explains. 'He can do his job at the back, come up front as well, and he knows that he has freedom to do both. That has made a big difference because the opponents' defence is not only focused on the two strikers, but they have to keep an eye out in case Patrick Vieira is coming. Who will mark him? There is a lot of confusion. He's a great player, so much strength and power at that age. And now you can see even the defenders are attacking and trying to do things with the ball.

As a defender you don't have to feel, *I'll leave the attacking to Ian and Dennis*. That will change more in the future as well so that Arsenal can be a better team. Even if they are just up there it helps us a lot. I can improve more and Ian can improve more.' Heck, how much more excitement can Highbury take?

★

Dennis van Kickaball, in his second season in the Premiership, is in masterful form, displaying tenacity to match his exquisite technique. That George Graham notion about performing stars is embodied in Bergkamp. He reaches a level of consistency which leaves onlookers rubbing their eyes in disbelief as, each week, he looks not merely as good as the last, but better. The North London derby provides the perfect opportunity for Dennis to silence the Eurosceptics, proving that foreign players can fuse staying power and lasting desire with their exotic skills. The Dutchman had been unaware of the peculiar potency of the fixture until his arrival at Highbury. 'To be honest I didn't know it was a special derby between Arsenal and Tottenham because there are so many clubs in London. I soon found out it was *the* derby. You notice that, not only from the players but from people on the street. It's bad when they are a Tottenham supporter, I'll put it that way. Then you know this is real rivalry.' Some decipher the ice-man, ever cool and composed, as lacking passion. Not so. He relishes the spectacle and the fever – traits which attracted him to English football in the first place – but his intensity burns quietly within.

The game has all the components fabled to shove foreigners off their stride. Aggressive and fiercely physical, way over the speed limit, a skiddy surface bombarded by teeming rain. 'For me it had the right ingredients, it has to have tension,' says Dennis. He shines. He shows there is a place for subtlety amidst this sizzling confrontation. When Merson hooks a pass into his path in the box he only has eyes for the ball. Wilson tangles with him and the pair fall to the ground, but Dennis, magnetic stare still fixed on the loose ball, bounds to his feet. The hapless Wilson tugs him back. Penalty. Bergkamp, spot-kick expert during his time with Ajax, Inter and Holland, leaves the task to

185

Arsenal's designated taker Wright. Anyway, the Dutchman adheres to a rule that if you get fouled yourself, you don't strike the penalty. 'Maybe if we were 3–0 up, but normally, no, I wouldn't take it,' he admits. Wrighty does his special routine and bangs the ball past Ian Walker, then struts around, his T-shirt shouting sweet nothings to his colleagues, and to the millions watching on television. *I love the lads.* 'We're a tight group with a lot of team spirit,' divulges Dennis bashfully.

On the hour Vieira lies injured so Arsenal kick the ball into touch for him to receive treatment. Tottenham's interpretation of fair play means Nielsen throws the ball straight into Lukic's box, but it's an attack rather than a sporting gesture to return the ball to the goalkeeper. Sinton pounces to plant the ball past Lukic and Highbury is in uproar. 'At that moment we were so angry,' claims Dennis, 'but we had time to settle it.'

The timing resonates with the never-say-die values of Arsenal of old, and the goal radiates with the vibes of Wenger's New Arsenal: in the 88th minute, reading the game one step ahead of every Tottenham man, Dennis anticipates the ball floating towards him, anticipates Tony Adams's run, then with the deftest of strokes he flicks the ball so that it drops perfectly onto the captain's boot without interrupting his momentum. Tony rattles a left-foot volley home. Dennis titters at the notion that such an elegantly fashioned, beautifully executed goal polished off by a centre-half is a new experience at Highbury. 'That's confidence. When defenders come up they can do the things attackers are doing.' And what about you in defence, Dennis? 'We always have that thing where we want to take on a player, and when you're at the back and you take on players, it's silly.'

Meanwhile, 2–1 in stoppage time and the fans are going bonkers. They are dancing in the aisles as Wright shimmies and soft-shoe shuffles by the corner flag. He sways this way and that, teasing the beleaguered Wilson who has no idea what Arsenal's loverman is doing with the ball. Ian looks up, spies Dennis ghosting into the box, and sends an enticing cross to his other half. One touch of Bergkamp's left foot brings the ball under instant control. One touch of his right and the ball hums into the net. One explosion of wonderful fervour, as he glides along the grass on his knees, arms raised, screaming. The euphoria the fans felt after Tony's goal cranks into hysteria. When you get two goals coming so close together your head spins dangerously out of control. And 3–1 as well, that scoreline so deeply embedded into the derby history. It's moments like this that people who don't like football never understand.

'I never expected the cross,' says Dennis. 'I didn't know how long Ian had the ball in the corner, but it was a great cross anyway. I only had one thing on my mind and that was finishing them off. Winning the game against Tottenham in the last two minutes was great. Looking at it both ways, as the game itself and as the Arsenal v Tottenham atmosphere, it was one of the biggest matches of the season. It was incredible because everything came together. I came to England because I wanted to experience the atmosphere which I think is unique in Europe. It's spectacular, there is always something in a game. Even if it's 3–0 it's never over. That's nice not only for a fan but for a player as well. It suits my game because it's always positive, on and off the field. The crowd expect attacking football in England and they don't in Italy because they play only for results. They would settle for a draw sometimes. In the last ten years Italy was the best league but to be honest I think it's changing now. England is very strong.'

After all the difficulties surrounding Wenger's arrival, the derby cements the manager's rapport with Arsenal, and it is symbolic of the ideals he wants to stamp on the team: the scope to play attractive, penetrating, winning football allied with slick organisation and powerful spirit. 'That's the way he wants to play,' confirms Dennis. 'If you look at the team, their experience and defensive record was there for so many years, and if I and some other players can add something to the offensive it will be a complete team and this was one of the games when we really showed that. The defence was very strong and offensively we were up there with four or five players. Total football as they call it in Holland, it was brilliant.'

Any new manager needs to win the faith of his players to get the maximum response. The three goalscorers, Wright, Adams and Bergkamp, are all influential characters in the squad who can affect the mood of the group as a whole. It speaks volumes for

Wenger the manager and the man that he so swiftly gained un-
stinting support from one and all. Not that it was a universally
straightforward task. Ian was easy, only too eager to please having
been released from his depression under Rioch; Dennis, an ad-
mirer of Bruce, reacted in his usual professional way and soon
enthused to the new man; but the skipper was dogged by doubts.
'As soon as Arsène arrived, there was a fear of someone else, the
fear of change,' Tony recalls. 'Who is he? Is this person going to
like me? No, he's rubbish, he's French – the newspapers obviously
loved that – and no foreign manager has had success in this
country. I've had Stewart Houston, Pat Rice, we're good pros
anyway, let me have the job. Pathetic things, really, but those
were thoughts that came through my head. Contempt before
investigation – that was my theory on Arsène. You've got to really
focus through all that and think, *Give the bloke a chance*. Who is
he? Talk to him. Get out there. Have a look at what he's doing.

'The time he actually won me over was about a month after
he arrived and I was still walking around with the hump. He
spoke to me and he was honest and genuine and I responded and
told him my reasons, my fears. It was very simple, very quick, but
it was just what I needed. As soon as you've won the captain over
you've got a hell of a chance with the rest of the lads. That's the
beauty of this wonderful life we've got here. I'm sure he never
went out to impress me or win me over; he showed me that he's
competent, intellectual, educated, he knows the game inside out,
and I've showed him that I want to play for Arsenal Football
Club and I'm trying to do my best, I'm playing with bloody
injuries but I'm there for him. I've got total respect for him like
I think he has for me.'

With Tony enlightened as a person and set free as a footballer,
with Dennis enjoying the English life and the English game as if
he's in his element, with Ian continuing to chalk up goals and
effervesce with the wildness of a child, Wenger's approach is hitting all the right chords. 'He's made me feel like I love the game
again,' chimes Ian. How different it could have been. Contem-
plate Wright's transfer request, and Adams' cold feet at the beginning of the season. Both now feel relieved they stayed. As for
Bergkamp, he feels so comfortable at the club he signed an

extension to a contract which already has two years to run. And in these Bosman days, with the financial incentives available to the cream of the world's talent, that's a mighty commitment.

★

Going into his third year at Arsenal, a season which culminates with the World Cup, Dennis is three goals away from Holland's all-time goalscoring record held by Faas Wilke. 'If I can achieve that it would be something like a medal,' he opines. Quite an accolade for someone who, barring injury, could have another five years at the highest level. It's even more impressive for someone who isn't even an out-and-out striker. Scoring and creating are equal parts of Dennis's game. Just as stunning as his array of finishing skills (will he arrow it, bend it, volley it, caress it . . .?) is his repertoire when it comes to controlling and passing. He is a Nureyev on a football stage and his balletic balance allows him to coerce the ball as he chooses regardless of the attentions of some over friendly defender. His ability to make space, see space, find space on the field that few others are aware of sets him apart from the ordinary. Wenger, Arsenal's alchemist, finds ready-made gold in Bergkamp: 'He is one of the best five footballers in the world. He has everything a player dreams of having. His talent is so pure you just want him to have the ball, and we will try to get him more involved in the game, get better balls to him, so he can show his talent.' The manager views his best position as that of a 'free striker' so he can roam wherever he wants, enabling him to shoot, or create, at will.

'I like to do both,' says Dennis. 'I always think I am in between, not really a striker and not really a midfielder. When you play in between you have to be able to both score and supply. That's going well now but I always feel I need to score more and I need to supply the others more as well. That's another aim to achieve.' Such is his desire if he misses a chance or fails to craft an opening he goes away to think about how he can improve for the next game and he is regularly last off the training pitch. The ball is his ally, so he spends a good deal of time with it to make sure their friendship remains close.

His striking partner Ian Wright claims to be privileged to

work alongside the conscientious Dutchman. 'When people ask who is the best player I've played with, I'd say Dennis,' he drools. 'He is just absolutely world class, pure ability crammed into one person, and he has a great attitude to the game. We room together and we talk a lot about football.'

So, Ian, have you learnt anything from Dennis? 'In respect of shooting, when he shoots it's so crisp and clean all the time and he's so calm.'

And do you think he's learnt anything from you? 'Yeah, he got sent off against Sunderland.' Indeed, he can look after himself, and if going in with bite is called for, he will.

Dennis reveals this isn't the only Wright habit to make an impression: 'Ian is one of the best for having a killer instinct. If only I had something like that . . .' His tone is wistful, as if he honestly means it.

They say the best strikers hunt in pairs and the Bergkamp-Wright duo is a compelling combination. The ice and the fire, the refinement and the unpredictability. They are intrigued by each other's characteristics: Ian the hothead views his partner's cool mannerisms with admiration. Dennis the straight man regards his partner's erraticism as, well, something of a challenge. 'He's like Dr Jekyll and Mr Hyde,' he muses. 'The way he can change in a game is amazing. At one moment he's playing a bad game and then suddenly he's there and he wins the match for us. Or the other way around: he's playing well and then he reacts to the referee and gets sent off. It's part of his game. Most of the time it's easy for me to know what he's doing to give a pass to him because he always wants to go to the goal. Sometimes he's so excited he makes a lot of movements and then I don't know what to do. I pass to the left and he's off to the right, but those occasions are rare. Most of the time we understand each other.' He has a mischievous glint in his eyes, as if he's balancing seriousness and jocularity.

Dennis's demeanour is reserved, his humour subtle. What the English construe as detached for the Dutch is normal. He has no problems in the coarse comedy zone of the dressing-room, which is in sharp contrast to the more laid-back atmosphere in Holland and the more intense mood in Italy. He finds it most agreeable, in that understated, dry way of his. Until he gained his bearings at Highbury he didn't quip back, but now he confesses to giving out 'a bit of stick'.

The happiness he has found here validates his hunch that Arsenal was the right move for him to relaunch his career after Inter. The ambience of the English game engages him, and away from it he is planting roots: his family are settled, his baby was born here, he doesn't ache to hop on the hovercraft back to Holland. 'I always feel when you're happy off the field you play better on it. It's important that when you play football everything is focused on the games, but for those four or five days a week when you don't play football it's equally important that you can relax with your family and don't think about football too much. That's what I find here. It's the culture, the way people live for football and want to be part of a team, but are also free to live outside. When you sign for a new club you never know how things will work out but, looking back, it was the right step for me and Arsenal.'

Bergkamp is in his prime, and upon such steady foundations he feels he has not only rediscovered his verve on the pitch but he hopes to augment it. 'In those two years in Italy I couldn't show my skills and qualities. I didn't think they played as a team in such a way I would do well. I was part of the team but they didn't see my strengths, they didn't understand. They just bought a player, Dennis Bergkamp, and thought *Put him in the team and we will win the league.* That won't happen. You have to play to my strengths and that's happening here.' He revels in being the kingpin, although having been brought up on the ethos of total football he's eager for a tad more parity to be spread throughout the team. The wind of change wafts through Highbury and whether Wenger's flurry of signings in the summer of 1997 sweeps the team up to his lofty standards remains to be seen. For Dennis, he knows Dutch team-mate Marc Overmars is a move in the right direction, and he's gratified months of hard persuasion at international get-togethers has paid off. 'I tried,' he grins.

We have reached a stage where, even though Highbury is sold out every week, the total gate money falls short of the players' wage bill. The club's new salary scale can attract precious talent which might have eluded them before. But Overmars, like Berg-kamp, didn't simply join Arsenal for the money – he could write his contract at virtually any club in the world. Neither did either of them come merely because they fancied London living. Over-mars, like Bergkamp, wants to win.

Two silverless seasons frustrated Dennis and fired his impetus to make a stronger challenge on the Championship. He needs to win medals to appraise his Highbury career as a success. 'Staying here for four or five years, if I didn't win anything, sure I'd have had a good time but I'd be disappointed,' he reflects. He wants to etch his name into Arsenal's history as a great winner as well as a great player, and as a man who helped unburden the club from its image of yesteryear with a flourish. The zeitgeist?

'When I came to the club, the period under George Graham closed. I heard the stories but I didn't really bother to ask anyone about it because it had nothing to do with me. I knew it was a successful time but I heard stories about Boring Arsenal and everything. It was in the past and I felt I was part of something new and I only wanted to concentrate on that. It's great that people, not only the Arsenal fans, but people all over the country and even in Europe, say it's really nice to watch Arsenal play. When I speak to people in Holland and Italy they say they really enjoy it. I understand that I'm part of that. I was one of the players who changed that. For the history, so far we have changed something in the style, but it would be better if we won some-thing. Then they can say Arsenal won the Championship, or whatever, and they did it in a way different to '89 or '91. That would be nice.'